THEOLOGY BY THE PEOPLE

THEOLOGY BY THE PEOPLE

Reflections on doing theology in community

EDITED BY
SAMUEL AMIRTHAM
AND
JOHN S. POBEE

World Council of Churches, Geneva

Cover design and photo: Rob Lucas

ISBN 2-8254-0862-X

© 1986 World Council of Churches, 150 route de Ferney,
1211 Geneva 20, Switzerland

Printed in Switzerland

Contents

A Prayer

God of life,
It is a daring thing for us to gather together to consider the theme
  "theology by the people".
How dare we do so, God, except that you invite us always
to *become*?
How dare we do so, God, except that you have already gone
before us, allowing your church to experience the invigorating effects of
  theology by the people?
How dare we do so, God, except that your methodology
includes listening, sharing and confronting?

And so we have come to this place in Mexico
We have dropped our administrative tasks,
our teaching assignments,
our research projects
and our local involvement in the struggle for peace with justice,
to examine all of these in the light of this theme.

Will you then not be with us, God?
Will you then not wrestle with us here in this place?
For we will not let you go until you bless us.
Gloria a tí Senor, gloria a tí
En el nombre del Padre, del Hijo y del Espiritu Santo,
Amen.

A.L. de Garcia

Preface

Ministry belongs to the whole people of God. Therefore, all God's people need to be appropriately equipped for ministry. The Programme on Theological Education (PTE) of the World Council of Churches has always emphasized this, and encouraged the churches to provide for it in their ministerial programmes. Various theological programmes have been devised to translate this principle into practice, and the response has been enormous.

In recent years, however, we have been witnessing a new phenomenon. People are not only eager to learn theology; they are also creating theology. This is happening all over the world — in basic Christian communities, house church groups, parish Bible study groups and in rural and urban groups committed to promoting justice and peace, freedom and human dignity. Ernesto Cardenal's *Gospel in Solentiname* provides an impressive example.

Christians who have never had access to formal theology are learning afresh to relate faith to life, worship to work, prayer to action, proclamation to protest, in new creative ways. They discover in that process that they are doing theology, and that they need theology in their search for new forms of Christian obedience.

As we recognize this new phenomenon, we gain new insights. People need theology and, more particularly, theology needs people. Theology needs the reflection of people committed to Christian practice to preserve its vitality and wholeness. The phrase "theology by the people" catches this insight and embodies this vision.

This volume contains the papers presented at the PTE-sponsored Mexico consultation on the theme, held in April 1985. They are not in themselves theological reflections by the people; they are reflections of theologians on "theology by the people". That does not call for apology.

The primary purpose here is to call the attention of theologians and those involved in theological education to take note of this new theological activity, learn from it and perhaps change their own ways of doing theology in the light of it.

"Theology by the people" focuses our attention on two aspects of the contemporary theological task. It seeks new ways of doing theology in community. It seeks also to see that an active commitment to justice and peace becomes an integral concern of the theological enterprise. The programmes of ministerial formation of the churches have to be reviewed and revised as to their purpose and style, method and content, in the light of all this.

I thank all those who have contributed towards this concern — and this publication. It is our hope that it will be followed up by further work on the theme. We hope to publish at a later date a collection of more theological responses — including those from church traditions not represented in this collection. We would also like to encourage the publication, primarily in local languages, of collections of actual stories through which people theologize.

Samuel Amirtham
Director, WCC Programme
on Theological Education

Introduction

From 14 to 18 April 1985 there gathered at the Centro Evangélico Unido (CEU), Mexico, some eighty to a hundred persons from around the world. They had come from Africa, Asia, Australia, America (North, Central and South), the Caribbean, Europe (East and West) and the Pacific. They were of different Christian traditions: Orthodox, Roman Catholic, Protestant and Pentecostal. They were church bureaucrats and executives, academics and pastors, lay and ordained, male and female, elderly and young, teachers and students. They had gathered under the auspices of the Programme on Theological Education (PTE) of the World Council of Churches (WCC) around the theme of theology by the people.

The second general secretary of the WCC, Eugene Carson Blake, once said that "the ecumenical movement is a result of concerns of ordinary church people who find their ecumenical aspirations limited by church structures".[1] The point is that the ecumenical movement gets nowhere unless and until ordinary church people are involved in it, embrace it and carry the torch of ecumenism. If the ecumenical movement is about summing up all things in and for Christ (Eph. 1:10), it is equally about the people of God whom God uses to effect that summing up of all things.

Blake's statement refers primarily to the ecumenical movement. But it has also relevance for the place people should take in church life. Here we may recall the Encyclical *Princeps Pastorum* which Pope John XXIII issued on 28 November 1959. In it he speaks among other things of the need for well-educated and well-informed local priests to cope with their environment. "But there is another need too... the equally urgent need for educating and training the laity of every nation not merely to be truly

---

[1] See "Eugene Carson Blake Dies, Was WCC Leader 1967-1972", *Ecumenical Press Service*, 85.CC.17.

Christian in their private lives but also to devote themselves to the work of the apostolate."[2] For good measure let us also recall some lines from Pope John Paul II's homily at the mass marking the beginning of his pontificate, on Sunday, 22 October 1978. He said: "The Second Vatican Council has reminded us of the mystery of this power (i.e. Christ's) and the fact that Christ's mission as Priest, Prophet, Teacher and King continues in the church. Everyone, the whole People of God, shares in this three-fold mission."[3] In so far as they share in that mission, they must also share in the theological task.

The statements of the two popes say a lot about the people's need for theological education and theology. But the statements do not appear to say enough about theology's need for the people — how the people do it and how it cannot be done without them and their perspectives. Nevertheless both statements are very significant. Both are from a church which holds fast to the Ignatian ecclesiology that "where the bishop is, there is the church". So the ordained person becomes very important if not the centre-piece of the church, with the people gathering around the bishop or his representative, the priest. And yet in that Ignatian theological context, the two popes emphasize the necessity for the unordained, indeed the *laos*, the whole people of God, to be educated theologically and equipped for their ministry in the world. Such an idea, of course, involves an ecclesiology which recognizes the church as the people of God, each segment of which is important for the "business" of the church, a community and communion in which the priests like the lay, the specialist theologians like the simple believers, the rich like the poor, are obliged by the word of God to reflect on and practise the faith and to profess and to give an account of the hope that the good news of Jesus Christ sets before humanity. It is this vision of the need of the ordinary people to be at the heart of the church's search for a meaningful and relevant self-under-standing and role in society and world, that is, in part at any rate, encapsuled in the rather clumsy phrase "theology by the people".

The ecclesiological implications of it, we shall return to later. Of course, common church people, the unordained, are not exactly the same as "people" in the phrase "theology by the people". For to say that it is necessary for the unordained to be educated and contribute to the church's life is not necessarily the same as to claim that the people are the subjects

---

[2] Text translated by Raymond Hickey O.S.A., *Modern Missionary Documents and Africa*, Dublin, Dominican Publications, 1982, p.147.
[3] *Talks of John Paul II*, St Paul's Edition, 1978, p.88.

of theology. Nevertheless a recovery of a sense of the church as the people of God is a prerequisite of it.

The point is sometimes made that the phrase "theology by the people" jars on some people, for diverse reasons relating to the words theology and people. For most people "theology" is the preoccupation of a specialist who expounds profound ideas which nobody but his/her kind understands; it is a discipline dealing with learned abstractions. As for the word "people" it conjures up ideas of simple, unlearned persons who allegedly can be manipulated by the learned. And to combine the two words seems, to some, an unequal yoking.

Expressions of theology by the people

1. Basic Christian communities

Strange as the phrase "theology by the people" may sound, it expresses an insight that is represented by *Comunidades eclesiales de base*, i.e. basic Christian communities, a familiar phenomenon in Latin America though found elsewhere, e.g. Holland, Italy, France. Partly under the inspiration of liberation theology, *Comunidades eclesiales de base* of liturgical and social life have grown up, particularly in Brazil. These are often loosely related to the parochial structures. They are, nevertheless, communities of women and men, ordinary people, who seek to live their Christian convictions in these communities, often because they feel the church has become part of the structures of oppression and also because of their dissatisfaction with the impartial and seemingly meaningless preaching of the gospel truth to all. Thus theology by the people has a major spring in the insights represented by the phenomenon of *comunidades eclesiales de base* and through that, liberation theology.

2. Minjung theology

However, there are other springs, particularly *Minjung theology*. *Minjung* is a Korean word. Etymologically it derives from the two Korean words, *min* i.e. people, and *jung* i.e. mass. Thus *minjung* means mass of people. Minjung theology is that reflection and praxis of the word of God by the mass of people. "Minjung theology is an articulation of theological reflections on the political experiences of Christian students, labourers, the press, professors, farmers, writers and intellectuals in Korea in the 1970s."[4] Minjung theology represents the political hermeneutics of the

---

[4] Arnulf Camps, O.F.M., "A Reflexion on 'Theology by the People'", *Ministerial Formation*, Vol. 29, March 1985, p.3.

gospel. To use the words of David Kwang-Sun Suh, a Korean theologian, "it (i.e. Minjung theology) is our effort to provide a framework of the political history of Korea and the socio-political biography of the Christian koinonia in Korea".[5] Minjung theology comes out of the biographies of suffering people. To that extent it is concerned with liberation from physical slavery and suffering as well as from political and economic exploitation.

3. African theology

In Africa today there is a tremendous development of African theology. African theology is concerned "to interpret essential Christian faith in authentic African language in the flux and turmoil of our time, so that there may be genuine dialogue between the Christian faith and African culture".[6] This may *prima facie* sound like an existing theology rather than creating theology from "below". But the impression is more apparent than real. For in so far as it uses folklore such as popular wisdom — proverbs, myths, songs, lyrics, rites and customs — as aids in interpreting the Christian message, it is developing a people's theology from below and by a route different from the Latin American route and, for that matter, the Minjung route. The rationale for this is *inter alia* that theology emerges from, among other things, a historical community and a people's experience. There is the implication that besides the biblical revelation which is rooted in Semitic and Greco-Roman cultures, there is also a revelation of God in traditional African wisdom and culture. Indeed, some would even claim that traditional African elements have much in common with biblical faith.

4. Black theology

Black theology, a type of liberation theology, is rooted in the black experience of slavery and economic exploitation, particularly in the United States of America and South Africa. It is a theological reflection that springs from the experience of people of black pigmentation who are discriminated against and oppressed in diverse manners. In that context, "revelation to the blackness is a revelation of Black Power, which includes black awareness, black pride, black self-respect and a desire to

---

[5] "Minjung and Theology in Korea", in *Minjung Theology, People as the Subjects of History*, ed. Kim Young Bock, Singapore, Christian Conference of Asia, 1981, p.19.
[6] John Pobee, *Toward an African Theology*, Nashville, Abingdon, 1979, p.22.

determine one's own destiny."[7] Its components are the black experience, the black theological heritage and the Bible. Thus here too the perspectives of black peoples at the bottom of the heap become a critical ingredient in theology.

5. Feminist theology

Feminist theology begins with the assertion that women's lives are fundamental to the enterprise of theology. It seeks to create theologies shaped by the heretofore unacknowledged — in the Christian tradition — experience of women. As a form of liberation theology it questions the very epistemological foundations of theology itself. In that questioning there arises the possibility of transforming theology. Feminist theology is re-examining the Bible and the history and tradition of the church from the perspective and perception of women.

Feminist theology is contextual and concrete; it is a theology which understands daily life to be the place where the manifestation of God occurs. It is marked by humour, joy and celebration and it is filled with a spirituality of hope. It is personal and communal; personal in the sense that it begins with stories of individual women's lives, and communal in the sense that theology arises in response to the shared stories. In feminist theology there is a constant breaking apart of the old patriarchal categories and systems in order that a theology closer to life may come into being. Indigenous forms of such theology have appeared in Latin America, Asia, Africa and other parts of the world.

Thus "theology by the people" is neither a new fad nor a new creation. It is already happening in Latin America as in Europe, in Korea as in countries in Africa. It is a necessary corollary of the rediscovery of the biblical affirmation of the priesthood of all believers. The author of 1 Peter, addressing "God's elect, strangers in the world, scattered throughout Pontus, Galatia, Cappadocia, Asia and Bithynia..." calls them "a chosen people, royal priesthood, a holy nation, a people belonging to God, that you may declare the praises of him who called you out of darkness into his wonderful light. Once you were not a people, but now you are the people of God" (1 Pet. 2:9-10). The church as the whole people of God has a duty to proclaim the good news and, to that extent, they need faith and praxis, both of which involve levels of reflection. If,

---

[7] Deotis Roberts, *Black Political Theology*, Philadelphia, Westminster Press, 1974, p.80.

indeed, every believer in Christ has a ministry to offer sacrifices and prayer and to present and explain the word of God, then all must be equipped for it. It is not only that everyone has a duty to theologize but that that is best done in community and while living together in faith. Theologizing is possible, nay, a duty even, outside the elitist group of professional theologians. "The Church can become a positive educational force in society if it allows the gifts of all the people to be used... A people's theology is a way of understanding God in the context of the everyday experiences of ordinary people. It is an active theology since it allows the whole group or community to make discoveries; no one person leads or teaches, all are learners and teachers. All questions are important enough to answer; no question or person is ridiculed. Outside resources such as experts or books are consulted only when the group sees the need. People's theology challenges us to live our faith more fully and more shared. It is a theology that comes from the people, in the language of the people, and in the service of the people." These words from *Work for Justice*,[8] a publication of the Transformations Resources Centre, Maseru, Lesotho, Southern Africa, sum up well what the various types of theology by the people are about.

Definitions

1. Theology

The expression "theology by the people" raises the problem of an adequate definition of theology. It can, however, be asserted that as a matter of fact there does not appear to be one correct definition of theology to which all can and should conform. So it is a hopeless task to attempt a definition. However it is defined, theology is concerned with constructing and articulating a faith by which people can live. Such theology should involve a praxis, i.e. a learning to live by the faith which they construct and articulate. Theology, properly understood, is born out of the interaction between critical reflection and praxis which is committed action. For, indeed, it is in that committed action that people may begin to understand the real meaning of their faith. There is a hermeneutical connection between faith and obedience, reflection and action. Reflection and praxis together belong to theology. Indeed, it is in the praxis that people come to the deeper understanding of the faith they profess.

---

[8] No. 28, August 1985, p.4.

2. *People*

What about the rather familiar and yet confusing word "people"? In some parts of the world which have experienced the tyranny and dictatorship of the masses, the word carries with it very negative connotations and populist overtones. Tyranny is not a necessary part of the content of the word "people", and certainly not in this context. But abuse does not do away with true use. Equally true is the difficulty of giving precise content to the word "people". However, "people" need not be exclusive. In the context of "theology by the people", the phrase does not seek to exclude the professional theologian — he/she is among the people. What the theologian does is *in the context of* and *with* the people, not *for* the people gathered as a community of faith. But who are the people?

As is often the case with familiar words, there is no one meaning. Various meanings are given: the poor, the oppressed, the marginalized, the suffering. As used in the phrase "theology by the people", it is not just a class term. For example, the Minjung of Korea include Christian students, labourers, press men and women, professors, farmers, writers, intellectuals and theologians. However, in defining it in the Korean context, one essential quality of people is the notion of *han*, a Korean word which means grudge or resentment. The Minjung are characterized by the feeling of suffering of a person who experiences repression and/or oppression. It can manifest itself as dejection, resignation, impotence and helplessness. Such people are aware of the contradictions of the situation marked by their unjust treatment at the hands of the powerful. But they by no means passively accept their sufferings; they strive to change the structures of oppressive society and culture through participatory democracy. An equally important idea relating to Minjung is the idea of *dan*, i.e. cutting off. The word "means different things to oppressors and oppressed. To the oppressor it means that they should stop being greedy and oppressive. To the oppressed it means that they should stop wishing (the oppressor) to be their masters and wanting to take revenge. Neither is easy to accomplish."[9] Again, in Korea the Minjung have reflected on their circumstances and identified themselves with the suffering servant and with the *ochlos* (Greek for crowds) i.e. common people and God's people of the story of the Exodus.

In the Latin American context, the word "people" has *sometimes* been abused. "The people are used and manipulated in a demagogic manner.

---

[9] Cyrus Hee-Suk Moon, "Minjung Theology: an Introduction", *Pacific Theological Review*, Vol. XVIII, No. 2, 1985, p.10.

The most fascist philosophies can pass themselves off as 'popular'. At the present time in Latin America the concept (not the reality) of the 'people' is being skilfully or ingeniously manipulated by certain outsiders or rightist groups, who are not on the side of the people, but are the ones who are plunging them into poverty. As an ideological cover, a certain 'philosophy of liberation' bolsters the policy of poverty. And as an orchestrated accompaniment pastoral theology holds up popular religion as the Latin American form of encountering God: 'We must begin with the people'... 'We must interpret the people'."[10]

However, abuse aside, there are more respectable uses. In Latin America the word refers to the "people of God". But people of God is not initially tied to its biblical roots. "We link it instead to the issue of democracy. In the concept of 'people', we are evoking a real power. We as Latin Americans are seeking to be people in whom popular power is constituted and established as collective will. In our history anti-people institutions have prevailed. Colonialist minorities, enslavers and capitalists imposed themselves, and continue to assert themselves against the indigenous people,... against popular will."[11] Against that background Latin Americans tend to conclude from the biblical references to "people" or "people of God" that "the people of God is constituted starting with the poor. Impoverished women and men are not one fragment of the people, beside which exist others similar to them. The 'people of Yahweh' is condensed into the poor, the church of Jesus. Nobody is excluded by this. But the centre around which the whole subsists is the poor"(*ibid*).

3. The poor

In the Latin American context there is this related term: the poor. Poor is almost synonymous with, if not identical to, the people. The concept of "people" presupposes the preferential option for the poor as is typically stated by the 1979 Latin American episcopal conference at Puebla. "The exact meaning of this option is to recognize the privileged status of the poor as the new and emerging historical subject which will carry on the Christian project in the world. The poor, here, are not understood simply as those in need; they are in need but they are also the group with a historical strength, a capacity for change, and a potential for evangeliza-

---

[10] Severino Croatto, "Popular Religion: an Attempted Statement of the Problem", *Ministerial Formation*, 29 March 1985, p.18.
[11] Milton Schwantes, "Biblical Theology Together with the People: Preliminary Notes", paper read at Mexico consultation (see chapter IV).

tion. The church reaches out to them directly, not through the state or the ruling classes. Thus, we are no longer speaking of a church *for* the poor but rather a church *of* and *with* the poor. From this option for and insertion among the poor the church begins to define its relationship with all other social classes. It does not lose its catholicity; its catholicity becomes real and not merely a matter of rhetoric. The church is directed towards all, but begins from the poor, their desires and struggles. Thus arise the essential themes of the church: social change creating a more just society; human rights, interpreted as the rights of the poor majority; socio-historical freedom and concrete service on behalf of the disinherited of this world, and so on."[12] Theology by the people then is a plea for the reflection on the eternal word of God to take seriously, if not start from the perspective of, those in the underside of history. For after all, Jesus did not come to give comfort to and affirm the rich and powerful; he was anointed "to preach good news to the poor... to proclaim freedom for the prisoners and recovery of sight to the blind, to release the oppressed, to proclaim the year of the Lord's favour" (Luke 4:18-19). Besides, Jesus said that "whoever wants to be great must be your servant, and whoever wants to be first must be the willing slave of all" (Mark 10:43-4).

No discussion of people can afford with credibility to be silent on two historic uses of the word "people" in this century. We refer to the concept of *Volk* (German: people) in Nazi Germany, and in the Nederduitsche Hervormde Kerk (NHK) and the Nederduitsche Gereformeerde Kerk (Dutch Reformed Church —DRC), both of the Republic of South Africa. The *Richtilinien* of Deutsche Christen, a Nazi group in the German churches, stated on 26 May 1932: "We wish that our church in the decisive struggles for our people (Volk) 'to be or not to be' fights at the head... We wish for an evangelical Church which is rooted in the nationhood (Volkstum), and we reject the spirit of a Christian cosmopolitanism (Weltburgertum)." They sought to create a synthesis between the German nationalist ideology and Christianity. "The purpose of the German National Church will be to make clear the deepest mission of Germans, the German nation... know that you are Christ's people! In other words, become for the nations the way home to the Eternal Father!"[13] In the process the "people" became an anthropological concept

---

[12] Leonardo Boff, *Church, Charisma and Power*, London, SCM Press, 1985, pp.9-10. See also John Eagleson and Philip Scharper, *Puebla and Beyond*, Maryknoll, Orbis, 1979, pp.264ff.

[13] Cited in Klauspeter Blaser, "The Barmen Declaration and the Present Theological Context", *The Ecumenical Review*, Vol. 36, No. 3, July 1984, p.301.

rather than a theological or even sociological concept. *Volk* was more the nation (Latin: *natio*) than crowd (Latin: *plebs*). This influence went over to South Africa where the people became the Afrikaaners.

In view of some unfortunate associations of the word "people" throughout history, it is important always to take seriously the Latin American provenance in the phrase "theology by the people". "People" in this context is not the same as the German *Volk* or the French *peuple*. The English word has varied meanings: persons, a multitude, lay persons. But when used in the Latin American theological context, *pueblo* refers to the poor people, especially the oppressed, exploited, suffering people. But it is more than the oppressed, exploited suffering people. People refers to more than the oppressed classes; it is a social block of the oppressed of the nation.

4. The preposition "by"

The difficulty of giving precision to the term "people" is perhaps not as disastrous as it sounds at first. If "theology" and "people" are important, equally important is the preposition *by*, according to the Latin Americans. "'By' indicates a productive cause, the very origin of the discussion. It does not mean that it is the starting point of a reflection *by* the theologian or the object, or the receiver or the medium through which it takes place. It has to do with the fact that poor people are the very origin of the theological discussion; so that the role of the theologian is reinterpreted as an 'organic intellectual' of the very people who are poor. The change of subject means that inasmuch as the professional theologian is the subject of theological production, this now passes on to the people themselves."[14] This, however, does not exclude the possibility that the church, the people of God, may delegate the task of theology to the professional in the spirit of division of labour and not as making the professional theologian the source of theology. The source of theology is the word of God.

Assumptions of "theology by the people"

There are some theological assumptions, in the areas of ecclesiology, Christology and revelation.

---

[14] Enrique Dussel, "Theology by the People", *Ministerial Formation*, Vol. 31, September 1985, p.5 (see Chapter I).

1. Ecclesiology

The phrase is unexplainable apart from the idea that the church is the people of God. The church is first and foremost a community, a people called into being by God through the proclamation of the word, and the sacraments. This is a clear shift from the Ignatian model that "where the bishop is there is the church", i.e. the church is the people of God gathered around their bishop at worship. The difference between the two ecclesiologies is the emphasis given to the bishop. In the Ignatian model the emphasis is on the bishop, an emphasis that has led to clericalism and a certain over-emphasis on rites and sacraments. But the ecclesiology presupposed by the phrase "theology by the people" emphasizes the essential community nature of the church as is confirmed in the biblical images of the body, the koinonia and the famous Petrine passage (1 Pet. 2:9ff.) cited above (cf. Matt. 18:20). To that extent "theology by the people" rediscovers an early Christian ecclesiology. But what are some of the implications of this rediscovery?

a) Ecclesiological value of people: If the church is the people of God, then it follows that the people who have responded to the word of God and appropriated the grace of God through sacraments have their own ecclesiological value in recreating the church of God. Each person among the people of God has a responsibility for propagating the gospel and reappropriating and keeping alive the faith once for all delivered to the saints. Spreading the gospel and keeping the faith alive can never be the preserve of the clergy and the professional theologian; all, clergy and the non-ordained alike, are entrusted with the task of fulfilling by word and deed the mission of the church. To that extent, theology by the people is about equipping the people of God, the new Israel, delivered and redeemed "to be a light to all peoples, a beacon for the nations" (Isa. 42:6).

b) People directly sharing in Christ: There is the conviction that each and every member of the people of God shares directly in Christ. Important as the ordained may be, they may not be regarded as the individual mediators of Christ. Indeed, as scripture and the liturgy put it, the only mediator and advocate is Jesus Christ (1 Tim. 2:5; Heb. 8:6; 9:15; 12:24). Of course, by this theology another model is being preferred to the long-standing Ignatian model. According to Ignatius, bishop of Antioch (A.D. 107-110), "the bishop is the figure who guarantees the harmony of the church by gathering it around him to celebrate eucharist, and thus eucharistic harmony is the assurance and expression of a true harmony with the will of God, or the 'mind' of God as embodied in

Christ".[15] That was the monarchical model of the church. "Theology by the people" implies a fraternal and communitarian model. The clergy have a responsibility with other members vis-à-vis church order, but they are not the church. The church is the community of the faithful, as indeed the early church taught. It is a community of love. But the idea of the bishop guaranteeing harmony between the different charismata is not necessarily in conflict with a fraternal and communitarian model, although in history there has been a tendency to contrast them.

c) Protest against clericalism: Theology by the people implies a protest against the clericalism of the church. Here there is an implied linking of clergy with theology, even though not all clergy are theologians. But the fact is that in many places the clergy have become the repositories of the church's wisdom. Magisterium that belongs to the whole church has been limited to the clergy. Hence the protest. The church as the people of God encompasses clergy and unordained together, in short, all who are united by faith and baptism. The type of relationship that should exist between the clergy and the unordained is stated by the Vatican II *Dogmatic Constitution on the Church, Lumen Gentium* (November 1964) as follows: "In the Church not everyone marches along the same path, yet all are called to sanctify and have obtained an equal privilege of faith through the justice of God (cf. 2 Pet. 1:1). Although by Christ's will some are established as teachers, dispensers of the mysteries and pastors for others, there remains, nevertheless, a true equality between all with regard to the dignity and to the activity which is common to all the faithful in the building up of the body of Christ. The distinction which the Lord has made between the sacred ministers and the rest of the people of God involves union, for the pastors and the other faithful are joined together by a close relationship... And so amid variety all will bear witness to a wonderful unity in the body of Christ: this very diversity of graces, of ministries and of works, gathers the sons of God into one, for 'all these things are the work of the one and the same Spirit' (1 Cor. 12:11). As the laity through the divine choices have Christ as their brother, who, though Lord of all, came not to be served but to serve... they also have as brothers those in the sacred ministry. As St Augustine very beautifully puts it: 'When I am frightened by what I am to you, then I am consoled by what I am with you. To you I am the bishop, with you I am a Christian. The first is an office, the second a grace; the first a danger, the second

---

[15] Rowan Williams, "Ignatius of Antioch", in *A Dictionary of Christian Spirituality*, ed. Gordon S. Wakefield, London, SCM, 1983, pp.205-206.

salvation'... The apostolate of the laity is a sharing in the salvific mission of the Church."[16]

Let us hasten to add that *Lumen Gentium's* stress on equality does not necessarily contradict specialization. Its emphasis on the important role of the lay people in the church does not exclude the need for theological professionals. Nevertheless, the insights of *Lumen Gentium* must be read against the background of the realities on the ground on which the unordained have not been taken as seriously as they should. Thus theology by the people implies a renewed ecclesiology. But even then there is need for implied structures that allow for the exercise of adult responsibility by the unordained and clergy to be allowed to work.

d) Taking seriously the agenda of the world: Theology by the people implies a church that takes seriously the agenda of the world in the light of God's word. The people, as defined above, are the ordinary people of the earth, the poor who are engaged by God's word. "It is a church of the people, with the values of the people, with their language, liturgical expressions, and popular religiosity."[17] But this is not a place for an uncritical faith, for insofar as the faith is about Christ crucified and raised from the dead, and demands a change, it is subversive in generating impulses for creating a new humanity and a new world. "That fact (of the opposition between people's religion and official religion) is of real importance in creating a theology beginning with the people, i.e. with their religious experience. Their experience is the basic element in popular religion. It is a real living experience of the numinous. The same could not always be said of official religion. Thus, when the people share in a process of liberation on the basis of faith, they have a hitherto unknown *experience* of the numinous, which inevitably flows back to give new content and form to their religious symbols and customs. There will still be popular religion — which is natural and healthy — but it will not be an escape from history, but will be incorporated into a historical process of liberation."[18]

e) Presupposition of the experience of people: Theology presupposes the experience of people. The experiences of people in their struggles against injustice and oppression, through which they begin to articulate

---

[16] See *Vatican Council II*, ed. Austin Flannery, Collegeville, Liturgical Press, 1980, "Lumen Gentium" 32-33, pp.389-390.

[17] Boff, *op. cit.*, p.34. There may be a problem of translation here. In English the phrase "popular religiosity" is rather dismissive. But in Spanish it refers to the religious instincts of the people.

[18] Croatto, *op. cit.*, p.25.

the meaning of faith, are important. A theology based on such experiences helps to see the world as the real place of God's mission and ministry. The correspondence between the church and the world is located in the fellowship of suffering and in the common hope that the last word does not lie with death-dealing powers. The last word is located in the cross-and-resurrection of Jesus Christ. Any theologizing that loses sight of the social context of persons loses sight of the concrete existence of persons and, therefore, their true personality. And there is no way in which human existence can be considered without addressing structures, be they social or historical. And words like freedom, peace, justification, reconciliation have social dimensions which no relevant theology can ignore.

2. Christology

Theology by the people implies a Christology if for no other reason than that the church is the body of Christ. Earlier on, the point was made that theology by the people involves the idea of the church of the poor and a servant church. That in fact is modelled on the example of Christ as the servant. The servant of God is the righteous one who accepted humiliation and suffering for God's sake. Three things need to be noted: the humiliation and suffering and apparent powerlessness that go with the ministry; the fact that such humiliation is not meaningless but a drama of humility and obedience to God, a mark of devotion to God, which sacrifices to the uttermost, even to death; and consequently the servanthood denotes special relationship between God and the servant.

The paradigm of humiliation and suffering is reflected in the life of the poor. Christ the servant is seen and affirmed in the faces of the poor. God's majestic fullness was and is found, nay revealed, in Jesus, born in the midst of squalor. The beauty of this God is to be discovered not only in things of aesthetic appeal but also in the face of an old toothless peasant woman, the despised and marginalized. As of old when the incarnation first took place, theology by the people with its preferential option for the poor implies a prayer to God "to give us eyes to discover you today, transfigured, in the midst of our world of poverty and of garbage, in our world of promiscuity, in our great winter, in our desolation... Maranatha... From our misery, along with all poverty we will be the focus of beauty capable of saving the world. If you look at us in our poverty, we will be the incarnation of the word and your beauty." These are words taken from the meditation by Maria Teresa Porcile Santiso, a Uruguayan, at the Mexico consultation. Theology by the people implies a

Christology which sees the Lord in the very frail and ugly spectre of human existence and, therefore, Christology is not understood in terms of power, but in terms of what is humble and fraily human. But such theology is also a call to make sacrifices on behalf of the poor, the weak. Power is seen in love and acts of love, not in status.

The servant Christology goes with the Son Christology. In the Bible the word "Son", or more fully Son of God, has a complex multivalent set of associations. And Jesus did appropriate that title. To be Son of God is to be dedicated totally to the purposes of God, even the suffering and death on the cross. To that extent sonship and servanthood overlap. The people, particularly the poor, are assimilated to Christ the Son — in them the Son is revealed to the world. The Lord is met in the hungry, the thirsty, the naked, the stranger, the imprisoned (Matt 25:31-46).

Those who have responded to the proclamation of the word and received the Spirit tune into Christ's sonship. As Paul puts it, "to prove that you are sons, God sent into our hearts the Spirit of his Son, crying 'Abba', 'Father'. You are therefore no longer a slave but a son, and if a son, then also by God's own act an heir" (Gal. 4:6-7 cf. Rom. 8:14-15). In other words, the Spirit of God's son calls in us Christ's own cry of intimacy and obedience. The Spirit of God becomes the spirit of adoption (Greek: *huiothesia* not *huiotēs*: sonship). This relates to the idea of theology by the people in two ways: (a) The vision of ordinary people contributing to the church's search for a meaningful and relevant self-understanding and role in society and world is, so to speak, appropriating and realizing in our own day the words of Jesus. "Father of heaven and earth, to you I offer praise, for what you have hidden from the learned and the clever, you have revealed to the merest children" (Matt 11:25). Second, adoption puts us into a family so that we can pray "Our Father". That goes with a sense of responsibility for other people in the family i.e. the believers and, we may add, the human family. The concern for human dignity of which justice is an instrument is precisely linked with the Christological and ethical implications of the prayer "Our Father".

3. Revelation

In principle the source of revelation is holy scripture. If that is so, then there is need for the specialist like the professional theologian as function-ary to have the freedom to speak over against the church. On the other hand, theology by the people would claim that the people's experiences also are a source of revelation. That is an implication of the preferential option for the poor. If that is so, then the question needs to be asked: what are the normative experiences. How does one judge between spirits? Or better still, it is important constantly to prove spirits made manifest in human structures. Walter Kasper has written words of caution in taking seriously people's experiences: "Tradition has constantly made this mistake and today there is a danger of making it in a different way; it could be by imperceptibly assimilating the Christian view of freedom to an abstract-liberalistic attitude or — on the other hand — by drawing up a 'theology of liberation' and at the same time — as occasionally happens — more or less imperceptibly making a Marxist-inspired situation-analysis the basis of theological statements."[19] In other words, while a relevant and authentic theology is practised in a particular temporal horizon, never shall its framework of reference forget its biblical and theological basis and direction and its transcendental dimension.

Implications for the practice of theological education

And what does all this mean for the practice of theological education? The success or failure of a church depends to some extent on whether the people of God do what they are gifted for. That presupposes that they have learnt what they should be and do and experience its truth. And that is where theological education comes into its own. Education in general is about revealing truth about human life and society. Through it society passes on its accumulated knowledge and insights to its members with the clear aim of enabling the community to continue with a certain quality marking their life. Thus where education is properly understood, it must be purposeful. Whatever purpose may be there, it must include ensuring the survival and continuance of the human community.

Theological education is for equipping the people of God to participate in God's mission. It seeks to motivate the people of God and through them all humanity to be redemptively involved in the world. Some routes to this goal are more visibly relevant than others. At times some routes may look useless, as in the case of some theological endeavours in the university tradition. As Michael Taylor puts it: "The university may pursue certain enquiries for its own sake or for nobody's sake and certainly not always for the sake of the people, but from which I nevertheless benefit and on which I am to some extent parasitic, as it investigates the texts and uncovers the content and nature of the Christian tradition and common wealth in a way for which I have neither the equipment nor the time but the results of which I am anxious to use... The

---

[19] *Jesus der Christus*, Mainz, M. Grünewald Verlag, 1974, p.243.

university may not always be as responsive to the church as one would like, dutifully setting about those tasks which the church judges to be most helpful at this particular point in its pilgrimage; but I am disposed to think at times it fulfills its responsibility by being somewhat irresponsible and producing material which is not what the church could have judged to be most relevant, so jolting its perspectives from an independent point of view."[20] But at the end of the day the vitality of theology is judged largely by its relevance to the life and tasks of the people of God.

This is where it is important to recall that education is qualified by the word "theological". The type of survival and continuance that is high-lighted is the theological — religious — one. It is different from social action but not unrelated to it; it is different from political action but not unrelated to it. H.M. Zorn has written: "Theological education is theolog-ical in the sense that it involves people in a commitment to mission and ministry, a commitment to the 'study of God' in the sense of his revelation in the life, death and resurrection of Jesus Christ and his continuous working through the Holy Spirit. This understanding of theological education involves an element that cannot be communicated by definition, by 'professional' training. Theological education that produces people without commitment has failed, whatever its academic and technical excellence may be."[21]

Scholarship in theology

At present the dominant ideas on the subject are very much Northern in origin, although Western education itself has been moulded by a complex of factors in history such as Islam, Christianity and materialistic aspira-tions. Two aspects of this tradition call for special comment here. First is its character of being tied to formal schooling so that the seminary or university becomes *the* place for theological reflection, in the process giving unwarranted primacy of place and authority to such institutions and treating them as the depositories of theology even when other non-formal institutions may be doing excellent work. Second is the fixation with a type of scholarship which glorifies academic and intellectual criteria and deifies hard intellectual work. This itself is a version of the notion of individual salvation which contrasts sharply with the com-munitarian ecclesiology mentioned above. The academic approach carries

---

[20] "People at Work — Some Consequences of Theology by the People for Institutions", *Ministerial Formation*, Vol. 31, September 1985, pp.34-35 (see also chapter XII here).
[21] *Viability in Context: the Theological Seminary in the Third World — Seedbed or Sheltered Garden?*, Bromley, Theological Education Fund, 1975, p.x.

with it a demand for scientific study, or in more exotic German parlance *Wissenschaft*, i.e. the systematic quest for ordered knowledge, proceeding by investigation, questioning and inquiry. Its methods include philological, historical, psychological, sociological, philosophical and other studies. This scientific method, especially after it received the imprint of the Enlightenment, has been by nature humanist and agnostic in tendency. Thus the commitment of Western theological education to the scientific method in its present form is in a sense a mixing of oil and water. But theological scholarship, properly understood, should operate in the areas of knowing, feeling and commitment, and as such should have a missiological thrust if it is to be accountable to the people of God and in their interest. Theology by the people, while not disowning scholarship, has the perspective that involves an engagement in the struggle for justice and the transformation of the world.

Theology by the people, precisely because of the implied ecclesiology, is committed to experiencing theological education as a community enterprise. Theology, to be true to its *raison d'être*, has to be in community; for it is the agency of the community of faith and the word of God.[22] It should not consist just of the professionals in a corner doing their own thing and using their own language. But the people of God as a whole, severally and individually, should make an input in the enterprise for their own sake as well as for the sake of the larger community. The nature of this input will differ. It always strikes one as odd that some young inexperienced person is adjudged an authority on the truth of the gospel simply because he/she has been to a seminary, when there are around old and wise persons. The wisdom of the non-professional should complement the technical knowledge of the theologically trained person. It is in mutual dialogue that both parties come to a clearer vision of what God is doing in this world today.

Here one touches on a real difficulty: the participation of the people becomes difficult if they have not been involved in formulating the policies and projects. Also the insights of the non-professional are not always dependent on some academic discipline because it can be argued that there is power in the biblical language which can create communication. Thus the Bible as source is presupposed.

---

[22] It should not be forgotten that there have been changes in the understanding of the scientific method. When, after the liberation from Spain, the University of Leiden in Holland, was set up in 1573, the intention was to raise pastors of the Reformed religion. It was then thought that the scientific study of scripture would guarantee the freedom of the word of God over against the domestication of the word by the Roman and other churches and by spiritualism.

Bible

Earlier on the point was made that relevant and authoritative theology is committed to the Bible; it is related to and measured by the gospel of which the Bible is a principal record. The Bible is always received as an interpreted text in the sense that each person in society reads it through his or her own eyes and spectacles of context which influences interpretation. Thus the use of the Bible must be from the perspective of the people, be they the Minjung or the poor or an ethnic group. The influence of context on interpretation does not entitle us to abandon the Bible. Exegesis becomes a hermeneutic spiral, i.e. a dynamic and creative tension and interaction between situation and Bible and vice versa, a tension and interaction which transcend themselves to reach towards a clearer vision of God who is at once in the context and yet stands above it in loving judgment. Besides, to avoid lopsided theology which is in captivity to a context, it is important for the reading of the Bible to be done in the context *as well* of the wider churches for mutual self-criticism and mutual enrichment. In other words, a people's reading of the Bible must be conscious of being a contextual theology, like any other theology, and be open to the insights of other contexts. This is very important especially because of the demonic use of scripture on occasions, such as the misuse of biblical concepts of people of God to justify and create wicked systems that dehumanize sections of the human community. The teaching of the Bible must be people-centred if it is to inculcate the insights of the Bible. "People are to be included in the process of interpretation. In other words, the teaching is a community affair, talking to each other, encouraging each one to bring his/her knowledge and views, moving from the known life-situations to the unknown, but in the direction of human transformation. Thus, for example, the fragile frame of the poor can become not only data to be reflected upon, but a vehicle of revelation, to carry Christ in his freshness, to reach towards human transformation. Further, teaching the Bible involves imaginative theologizing from the original context of the Bible passage to one's situation. That is not a novelty; it is following the logic of Jesus' style of teaching through the earliest disciples to our day."[23]

Contextuality

Theology by the people implies that theology is a second step, in the sense that it presupposes and is based on the life and commitment of

---

[23] J. Pobee and D. Bosch, "Bible and Human Transformation", *Mission Studies*, Vol. 2, No. 1, 1985, p.69.

Christian people. Thus whatever is represented by that word contextuality, it is a flag word of theology by the people. It is by design that we speak of "whatever is represented by the word contextuality". For that word today is used in many senses. Lesslie Newbigin has commented that "as now commonly used, it seems to me to refer to a kind of theology which starts from the problem which a community faces and then, with this predetermined framework, seeks to formulate the Christian message. The end result is inevitably a programme or a crusade rather than 'good news', law rather than gospel".[24] And so it is that some Latin American liberation theology has sometimes been, perhaps unfairly, accused of Marxism parading as Christianity. But despite such criticism the word contextuality was originally meant to be "that wrestling with God's word in such a way as to discern the particularity of this historic moment; and by contexualization we mean the wrestling with God's word in such as way that the power of the incarnation which is the divine form of contextualization, can enable us to follow his steps to contextualize".[25]

Every theology is contextual and, therefore, not neutral. The so-called "classical" theology is itself contextual, adopting very much Northern presuppositions and style. Describing it as "classical theology" is not to be sensitive enough to the plurality of departure or entry points to the theological enterprise. In any case contextual theological statements not infrequently lose their meaning as the context changes. Thus we cannot do theology for all people. Anything created in a particular limited context needs to be put in the context of the church universal for mutual affirmation and correction. Thus dialogue between contextual theologies is a non-negotiable part of doing theology in a world of peoples. In the dialogue there is no elite superior knowledge. Rather, each contextual theology brings yet another piece in the mosaic of theologies and peoples around the globe. Lacking even one piece, the beauty of the mosaic will never be revealed. But they must be in critical encounter.

Dialogue as a method

Dialogue implies commitment to an ecumenical theology. Theology by the people must be ecumenical. The dialogue should be at least of three types: interfaith dialogue, intercontextual and interconfessional. For example, within Africa the theologizing by the people must be interfaith.

---

[24] "Theological Education and Scientific Approach", *Theological Education in Europe*, Geneva, WCC, 1980, p.67.
[25] Shoki K. Coe, in *Theological Education*, Vol. XI, No. 1, autumn 1974, p.7.

The people have a culture which is a world-taken-for-granted, which they take in, so to speak, with their mother's milk. Whatever foreign influences may come along later, these can never eradicate the world-taken-for-granted. Therefore, a people's theology in Africa has no choice but to engage the traditional culture (including religion) of the place. Denunciation of traditional culture has proved to be an immature way of engaging the people. Therefore dialogue betwen the Christian tenets and the African culture should be a mark of the encounter.

At the same time there is need for dialogue between the confessional bodies, for they imply divergent ecclesiologies such as the Ignatian model and the congregational model. Equally important is the dialogue between contextual theologies. Neither synthesis by addition nor synthesis by reduction is based on a candid appraisal of realities. The only option left is dialogue between faiths, religions, theologies, etc.

Dialogue demands a number of crucial points. First there is the need for realism in taking into account the pluralism that there actually is, the particularity and peculiarity of each mosaic piece. In so doing the people in any other religion and theological stream are taken seriously as proponents of a particular theology. Second, such dialogue is conducted not only by the professionals but also, and perhaps more importantly, by people who are in their daily lives in meaningful religious co-existence. Third, such dialogue demands an openness as to what the end result may be. Fourth, dialogue demands respect for the other party whose belief is different from our own. This requires each one to reflect on whether there can be a norm in addressing diverse revelations. Fifth, for dialogue to be truly effective, there may be need for a place where the results of the dialogue are formulated and made applicable for church life.

Interdisciplinary theological education

Theology by the people has to be interdisciplinary. If, indeed, in the Christian tradition there are no sharp distinctions between the sacred and the secular, the eternal and the temporal, the spiritual and the material, religious and socio-economic and political tasks, then theology by the people must take seriously the social, economic and political realities of the people. The history and socio-political reality of the people become an important element in theologizing. There is a need to examine how religion may operate from a sociological analysis of the people's situation. Knowledge of the inner link between the individual and the social becomes important in theologizing.

The role of the professional theologian *inter alia* is to listen and show sensitivity to what the community is saying and experiencing and to articulate it for the community as a first tentative step till the community can do its own articulation. The professional cannot presume to write "theology by the people" in the sense that it is the people who do their theology. That is because they do not have in their bodies the experience of the poor. "But we can sense them, smell them, hear their cry and, who knows, be converted by them. We cannot certainly go to the heavenly banquet without them; we cannot certainly love as in the Song of Songs, without knowing that they are also loving through the same beautiful experience, we cannot rest on the Sabbath day without their rest, their joy, their renewed bodies."[26]

Let us return to the point made earlier, namely the Northern scientific method. The scientific method is committed to doing theology in terms of propositions and rationality. That should not be despised at all. But if theology is to be done by the non-professional, then its language will be that of the story which is very much the experience of the Minjung. "The act of telling the story itself and the contents of this particular story give an important clue to understanding the style of doing theology by the people."[27] The stories are told in socio-political-economic language in which they found socio-political praxis. Such theology then is "a body language; the total commitment to their theology became words in action. We saw our actions become events, and we reflected upon these events."[28]

While the so-called "classical" approach has been critical, analytical, deductive and propositional, theology by the people seeks to complement it by offering the language of images, especially in the context of cultures that are largely oral and non-literary. Besides, the Bible offers ample examples of the use of images of ordinary life to communicate the good news of Jesus Christ. Such language may strike some as too pedestrian. But the use of image language for communication preserves the twin elements of openness and hiddenness — which is after all what the mystery of the kingdom is all about. Besides, such image language is a lively process of seeing life with new eyes and, therefore, facing people more pointedly with the demands of the kingdom. In this way the people reappropriate the word of God.

---

[26] Jaci C. Maraschin, "Theology, Bodies and People", *Ministerial Formation*, Vol. 31, p.38.
[27] David Kwang-sun Suh, "Theology of Story Telling: a Theology by Minjung", *Ministerial Formation*, Vol. 31, p.13 (see chapter VI).
[28] *Ibid*.

Theology is knowledge, and more than knowledge. To know God as the Bible shows is not only intellectual knowledge but an engagement with life's struggles in the light of God's word. Theology is a call to holiness which is not to be confused with participation in sacralized routines. It is in this light that the exodus motif of the Bible, Old and New Testaments alike, has become central to theology by the people. Theology is about the reality, nature and scope of God's liberating activity. You do not only read it but you join in that activity of God for your time and place.

In the words of Elsa Tamez, a theologian from Costa Rica, "the fact that the marginalized sectors are doing theology, i.e. they are thinking about God from their own perspective and in their own way, (means) they *have made their faith a living faith*. Their theological reasoning, because it arises out of their own experiences, is more convincing... for their Christian life, because theological statements that do not arise out of real life have ended up by becoming facile phrases, empty of meaning. From the moment the people attempt to do theology, a spirituality bursts forth in which there is greater consistency between the daily life and the religious life. Finally, the fact that the people *say* their theological word and are heard signifies a step forward in the recognition of their dignity. When the hungry ask for bread and receive it, their dignity is not necessarily being taken into consideration. But when the people think and enter into theological dialogue, they recover their dignity (in their own way) and to make their contribution also implies the recognition of their dignity".[29] This is also a liberation exercise. In this regard, we may recall that a crucial normative theme of the word of God is the Exodus motif. The Exodus is the decisive event of the liberation. Revelation, salvation and redemption happen in the midst of human history, particularly in acts of deliverance and liberation, in the exodus of the oppressed and marginalized people from bondage to freedom.

Of course, it is easy for the engagement to become just a programme. The wrestling with the word of God must be in the Holy Spirit. As such, theology is learnt also on the knees. Meditation, reflection, quiet worship are essential mediating points creating the openness to theological sharpness. Theology by the people is communicated through liturgical forms as well. It is important to see worship not as an extra but as an integral part of theological search. Insisting on the basis of the Judeo-Christian tradition, as Ian Fraser puts it, "the Hebrew/Christian insists that you

---

[29] "A New Stage in the Development of Christian Community", paper submitted at Mexico consultation (see chapter XI).

cannot know God and God's purposes unless you spend life first following the light you see and only then seeking more light".[30]

Ongoing concerns

In the North as in the South, and perhaps more so in the South, there is
some quiet reformation taking place in church life and theology. A first
characteristic of this reformation is theologizing from below or the
underside of history, which is at once challenging and complementing the
predominant Western theology and the dominant theological education
patterns of the former colonial countries. These theologies from below,
revealing as they do the fundamental crises of the world, have a crucial
importance for the ecumenical movement. But how do we promote
dialogue between the two types of theologies so that they may continue to
challenge and complement each other? How do we promote these
encounters so that ecumenical theology may grow?

The second characteristic of these theologies from below is that they
are done in community. No longer may the professional theologian and
the ordained minister claim any monopoly on the production of theology.
People at the grassroots are reclaiming the right to theologize. They are
taking the initiative to do theology by themselves alongside the academic
theologian. Thus it is a reactualization of the biblical idea of the
priesthood of all believers. Here then is a challenge to the traditional
concept of ministry. Some questions are raised by this: Do the style and
structure of the ministry today enable the people of God to articulate their
faith on their own and in mutual and open participation? Does the
participation of the whole people of God visibly find expression in the
participation of women, men, children, the marginalized? Is the liturgy a
solo performance by the clergy? How can the liturgy be reformed so that
it affects the right of all people of God to exercise their ministry? How can
we change the structures of theological education so as to further the
cause of theology and ministry in the community? How can academic
theology and non-academic theology enrich each other?

There is another aspect of theologizing in community that needs to be
highlighted. Theology in community demands serious engagement with
the context. This theology cannot be legitimately done outside the context
of the sufferings of people and their liberative praxis. To that extent the
cross of Christ and the Exodus become important themes and paradigms of
theology by the people. By the same token, theology by the people is and

---

[30] Paper read at Mexico (see chapter V).

should be prophetic in the sense that it is critical of the death-dealing and destructive powers of the world. The implication is that faith and theology cannot be confined to "spiritual" matters but must claim the whole of creation and human existence for God. Therefore, we need a wholistic spirituality, a spirituality that can struggle for justice and present our total existence as an offering to God at the same time. What type of spirituality do we foster in theological education programmes? How can this spirituality vitalize our own learning and living in community?

The spirituality in which theology by the people is based is nurtured by Bible study. The rediscovery of the Bible, with the realization that it provides contemporary meaning for a life of faith, is a powerful instrument for renewing theology and the people. But in this task there is need for the people's perspective to be brought to bear on the exegesis. Such Bible study involves a creative dialogue between the gospel and the context. As such the exegesis is contextual and must engage other exegeses in the church universal. Thus theology by the people calls for a theology that is at once contextual and ecumenical.

We need to define the terms more sharply. The phrase "theology by the people", as pointed out earlier, can convey different meanings to different people. So the very phrase needs some definition. Here we have attempted to deal with some of the various usages. It is necessary to continue this process of definition.

At the Mexico consultation some tentative directions were indicated: (a) Theology cannot be an intellectual, scientific study only; it is knowledge as well as wisdom to live by in concrete situations. That is why it should emphasize the issue of peace with justice. For to know God is to do justice. (b) All theologies, even the so-called "classical theology" of the North, are contextual and need to engage and be engaged by each other. Thus the ecumenical perspectives on theological education must be vigorously pursued. (c) There is need to pursue the non-written expressions of the people's relationship with God and each other through prayers, forms of liturgy, styles of architecture, etc.

The term "people" as it is used now carries diverse meanings: all peoples, all baptized people, the poor. The Mexico consultation once more indicated directions to take. The "poor" are not only the economically deprived, but also those who are disenfranchised, the oppressed, the marginalized. In a sense, it is a representative term. No one is excluded, though some can exclude themselves. Since the biblical faith has a "preferential option for the poor", theology needs to work out the structures and implications of such an option in practical, everyday terms.

Another ongoing concern is to examine the implications of the concept of theology by the people for theological education structures. It involves both theological issues and structural issues. For example, how do we see the traditional school as complementary for the extension programmes? How do we resolve the seeming conflict between the two approaches? There is need to explore the structures for linking grassroots theology to academic theology. How do the specialist theologians help the people and how are they helped by the people so that all together can reappropriate theology, discovering God's word for the world today?

I

Towards a Clarification of Terms

Enrique Dussel

Theology by the people? This is not just an interrogation, it is a challenge, a questioning, and almost a utopia. Can the people make or produce theology? Who are the people? Is it possible to have a theology produced by the people themselves?

In this short introduction, I do not pretend to answer these questions. Rather, I will leave them open for debate.

Theology? Which theology are we talking about? Academic, scientific theology produced by the intellectuals of the profession? It seems that theology has been nothing but that: the work of specialists and the task of intellectuals. In this sense it would be difficult, if not impossible, for the people themselves to produce theology. Surely, we must understand it in a more profound way so that it can be an object of popular reflection as such.

People? In English, the word "people" is not the same as the German "Volk", the French "peuple" or the Spanish "pueblo". "People" can mean "persons", a "multitude", "lay persons" (the non-specialists in something). I would like to give it a particular meaning, the strongest one: "pueblo de los pobres", i.e. poor people, but even more so, oppressed, exploited, suffering people.

Even with the meaning of oppressed, the poor, "pueblo" has been interpreted by some as a social class: the industrial or rural workers, etc. That is to say, those who have salaries. However, "pueblo" is much more than oppressed classes, especially those in the peripheral, dependent nations of the third world. "Pueblo" certainly includes the oppressed classes, but it also includes many other social elements: ethnic groups

---

● Enrique Dussel teaches church history in Mexico. He coordinates the church history work of the Ecumenical Association of Third World Theologians.

with their own language, race and religion; tribes; marginal groups which are not even a "class", simply because they have not achieved a salaried position within a weak capitalism. Therefore, strictly speaking, "pueblo" is the *social block* of the oppressed of a nation. From this, firstly, we cannot identify "pueblo" with a "nation" or "people". When someone says "the people of India", we must distinguish between its *populist* meaning (all of the nation) and its *popular* meaning (the social block of the oppressed).

We wish to speak of theology "by the people", with the meaning of theological work by the "social block of the oppressed" in the nations of our present world, but very especially the "social block of the oppressed" from the exploited, peripheral nations of the third world. Here "poor people" is a suffering reality that cries aloud to heaven as in the time of Moses.

A new beginning

But there are other questions. Is theology the same if it is *from* the people, *for* the people, *in* the people or *by* the people? Certainly all of these particles have different epistemological meanings.

When the professional theologians realized that their theology was indifferent to the poor people, they wished to "come closer" to the people and began a reflection "from" the people. The theme was discovered by the theologian from the reality of the people. We could say that the theologian's "theme" came out of the reality of the people; they were pertinent and real problems.

Later another step was taken: a pedagogical and didactic system was created. They went on to theological "extension" — audiovisuals, comics, simple writings for quick consumption, with drawings. The "for" indicated who it was destined for.

Soon the professional theologian discovered that no matter what, he or she lacked experience, the popular experience. So some decided to go to the people and become a part of the poor people. In that closeness new dimensions were understood which they had never imagined before.

Anyhow, all of these attempts came forth from the theologian or theology (or the more "cultured" elements of the churches or their structures) *towards* the poor people to evangelize them, they would say.

We believe that the expression "by the poor people" indicates something very different, a breaking with the very subject of theology and a new beginning.

"By" indicates a productive cause, the very origin of the discussion. It does not mean that it is the starting point of a reflection *by* the theologian or the object, or the receiver or the medium through which it takes place. It has to do with the fact that poor people are the very origin of the theological discussions; so that the role of the theologian is reinterpreted as an "organic intellectual", or that very people who are poor. The change of subject means that in as much as the professional theologian is the subject of theological production, this now passes on to the people themselves. The first question is: Is this possible? Is it theology that is thus produced? If it is theology, what of professional, academic and scientific theology?

If "theology by the poor people" exists, this should always be a reflection. First, reflection about the Christian *praxis* of those very poor people. It is the concrete, historical, suffering praxis which is the object of this reflection, which as a second act makes the first act explicit: the praxis of the people. In Latin America, theology produced by the grassroots groups in the basic Christian community comes out of the praxis, from the experience of the very community.

The community (koinonia) itself and its praxis, then, are prerequisites for this theological reflection. Praxis is not only action; it is basically a relationship: a relationship of person-to-person. To be together in a community is the fundamental praxis that anticipates the kingdom of God. To gather together in God's name is the originating experience. Later many other types of praxis follow which are concrete, historical, from "breaking the bread" to helping the most needy and working for the cause of justice.

But to reflect on their own Christian praxis, the grassroots communities, the poor people must "recuperate" the word of God, the Bible, which has been "kidnapped" by the dominant structures of the churches and also by the theologians. This "recuperation" or recovery of the word, this "kidnapping" of the "kidnapped" Bible is the originating act and the condition that makes possible a "theology *by* the people". To recover or "counter-kidnap" the Bible means that the people themselves begin to create their exegesis, their interpretation, from their own viewpoint, from their spiritual experience of the kingdom, from their sufferings, but equally from their millennial "wisdom" (not necessarily uninfected by alienation — and thus we would have to discuss the prophetic criteria that the people themselves use to discern what they have of wheat and chaff among themselves).

Second, once the Bible has been recovered — which is a way of "knowing" the scripture in a new way — people must begin to know how to use the word in their community. It is not infrequently said that "masses who are silent and learn, as students, are the people: they are passive, do not express themselves. They do not have a voice…" But in community people begin to speak, to express themselves, to think out aloud. They also recover "their" word which, made fertile by the word of God, begins the long journey of what will become a "theology by the people".

The recovery of the double word permits the exercise of thinking from the faith, from the Bible, from praxis. But which praxis? It cannot be a praxis that promotes alienation, a praxis that repeats the system which oppresses it, a praxis which through domination has introduced itself into the people. It deals with a praxis of liberation, i.e. when the people stand up, when they protest, when they struggle for their rights, for participation, for democracy, for justice. When reflection of faith on a popular praxis of liberation occurs, the people *create* theology, produce a new theology which becomes transformed into prophecy.

Examples

Near Esteli in northern Nicaragua, I once had a conversation with friends and with communities. We were surprised by their repeated and creative use of certain books which were somewhat forgotten within theological tradition, especially Ezra and Nehemiah. After the Babylonian captivity (read Somoza and dependent capitalism), the basic Christian communities in the northern part of the country had the double function of the captives liberated by Cyrus (the Sandinistas?). First, it was necessary to reconstruct the "walls", the "walls" of Jerusalem. The wall was an instrument of war, of defensive war, that impeded the return of the previous dominators to oppress Judah. In the same manner, the basic Christian communities of northern Nicaragua were constructing their "wall" against the "counter-revolutionaries" who were attacking their northern border. To protect the northern border was to construct "Jerusalem's wall". A theological reading, reflection from the grassroots, discourse in faith which is at once coherent, historical, political and prophetic.

But at the same time the liberated captives constructed the temple in Jerusalem. And those Christians, gathered in their Christian community with the consciousness that it was there that they were building the Christian Temple with living stones.

In other Nicaraguan communities, on the other hand, they would read the stories from Exodus, but not pay such close attention to Moses' acts and the people of God up to the Red Sea; those were the struggles against the Pharaoh (who for them is Somoza). Now, in the desert, with Egypt behind them, but still with forty years before them to get to the "promised land," it was the time of temptation to idolatry. Did not Aaron worship an idol? Are there not by chance important ecclesiastical persons within Nicaragua who would like to return to Egypt? The poor people do not fear reconciliation and from their "concrete and millenial wisdom" "understand" the real and present meaning of the scriptures in a way that is impossible for a biblical "book worm". Do not those who are well want to return to Egypt? Some say that they went to Miami; they have left the desert, they could not "withstand" the sufferings, they did not like the "manna". And thus, the community rereads Exodus line by line, in the desert, to produce theology (from which the professional theologians will be able to drink abundantly if they decide to become "disciples" of the poor people).

In a basic Christian community in Brazil the Christians once again re-read the parable of the Good Samaritan. A man was assaulted by thieves who left him by the side of the road half dead. Two men go by and do not help him. Finally comes the Samaritan, who helps him. All of this is well known. The grassroots theological reflection, however, proceeds in a novel, creative way which breaks with tradition. They ask themselves: Who is that poor man, robbed and wounded? The professional theologian would have responded (looking upon the other as himself): "The poor; Jesus who identifies himself with those who are hungry." But the people respond in another way: "It is us!" The poor, robbed, half dead is the people themselves. A break with the subject, a change of perspective!

And who are the robbers? They are those who take our land from us, those who rob us by increasing the prices of food, the military which torture and assassinate us... And who is the priest who first went by? He is like those "priests" or "ministers" who talk a lot but do little for us. The man who came by next is like the politicians who promise a lot, but do not fulfill their word. And who is the Samaritan? He is like Monsignor Oscar Romero who really was on the side of the people, like Monsignor Casaldaliga, like those who help us with our cooperative. But the "theology by the people" has not finished its theological discourse. And they ask: "What must we do in the face of this?" And they reflect: "It is necessary for us to walk along the road like that man who was headed towards Jericho. We need to go to our work, to our home. We cannot cease to use the road. What will we do?" And they conclude: "That traveller was assaulted because he was going alone, he was just one person, that is why the bandits could assault him and leave him half-dead. Many of us must go along, many together, we must go well organized. That is, we must organize ourselves and do all things in community, together, so that what happened to that traveller will not happen to us."

A new possibility

Once the people have recovered the word of God, they make it their own. They do not become tied down to the pure exegesis of the scientist who only wants to know the content of the text "at that time". On the contrary, the people, with much more wisdom, appropriate the word, place it as a light for how the kingdom is "today" and have no epistemological problems in "continuing" the discourse of the same parable of Jesus *here and now*.

Not only has the subject been changed, but the discourse has been prolonged. Innovation, production, theological and spiritual creativity. What is this discourse? Is it theology? What is certain is that "theology *by* the poor people" is a new possibility for theology, it is a new theological age, it is a new hermeneutics, a new interpretation.

And scientific theology? Because it is such, does it disappear? Not at all. Scientific theology must now define its articulation with popular-theological production, if this latter is a reflection from a community which is the subject of a liberation praxis.

I recognize I have raised more questions than I have answered. But there are still more questions. How is that popular theology expressed? What are its instruments: the oral word, music, theatre, painting, dance...? How does this theology transmit its contents to the members of the community?

What is certain is that the basic Christian communities are *the place* of production, expression, communication, and it is not easy for the professional theologian to adjust to it if he or she has not been willing to listen to it and learn from it.

"Theology *by* the people" is carried on by the oppressed people, by the poor, by the suffering. It is a theology which reflects in a popular way the praxis, the experience of the people, who become the *subject* of theological production and not the object of theological *extensions* which do not belong to them (even though these foreign theologies come to them in a populist way).

"Theology by the people" is a challenge, a threat, a possibility, perhaps a utopia, but no matter what, a necessity.

II

Complementary Theologizing

J.N. Kudadjie

It is clear that "the people of God are the primary agents"—indeed, one may dare to say the only agents—"of the basic theological tasks of the church". For who can understand the mind of God or recognize God's purposes and interpret God's signs but the people of God? The theme and the intention cannot be questioned. They are relevant to our times—especially since in all aspects of life there is an emphatic demand for people affected or likely to be affected by any enterprise to be involved in the decision-making processes and the decisions taken! One is all too aware of the opportunities and advantages as well as the problems and disadvantages in the new trend. It is in this light that the following comments are made.

The participants in theology

The title "theology by the people" rather smacks of a reaction ideology which ironically does not include everybody, but effectively excludes some of the people. The expression "people" has come to suggest a dichotomy, indeed a conflict, between the "privileged" and the "deprived", especially in the new nations. There is a real danger, therefore, that the title—not the *theme*—may put off some people. Cannot a less ideologically loaded title be chosen—one that will guarantee the recognition as well as the *creative* and *corrective* involvement of *all* God's people?

The church—and the world—loses much when some insight has been consigned and condemned never to see light simply because it comes

---

● Joshuah N. Kudadjie is senior lecturer in the Department of the Study of Religions, University of Ghana. His field of specialization is moral philosophy. He is also the secretary general of the West African Association of Theological Institutions.

from the "uneducated". Yet, it is not all the people who can do theology; for theology is not just the reception of God's self-revelation; it is also the interpretation and the articulation of an understanding that one has of God's purposes and action. The reception itself may, more easily, come to all manner of people. Philosophers have rightly pointed out that immediate experience itself—such as my eyes seeing an object—is value-free and error-free. It is when I make a judgment or statement that I can see a white bond sheet of paper, that my experience is exposed and may inform or misinform. Visions and dreams in themselves do not mean much to a people until they express, interpret or act upon it by accepting its guidance or setting it aside.

On the other hand, one who has not had an immediate experience of something cannot very well describe it, however much one tries to imagine and conjecture. Experience plus description and/or interpretation must go together in order to give information. Doing theology, then, must include both experience and description or interpretation. This, again, endorses the theme. For while many a professional theologian may have the ability to describe and interpret, he or she may not have the experience—that is to say, may not have "Christian faith" upon which he or she is supposedly reflecting. Equally, many a faithful Christian may lack the gift or ability to articulate the understanding of God.

The Pauline "division of labour" and diversity of ministries could sanction the status quo: let us restrict participation in theology to the professional. Let the "ordinary people" be content with participating in homiletics. To do otherwise is to confuse theology (the systematic articulation of the faith community's encounter with and understanding of God's purposes) with homiletics (the plain exposition of scripture or exhortation based on it). There is a variety of ministries and offices and abilities and gifts. All are not apostles, or prophets; some are evangelists, some pastors, and others teachers. Christ did this "to prepare all God's people for the work of Christian service, in order to build up the body of Christ" (Eph. 4:11-12; 1 Cor. 12; Rom. 12:3-9).

However, we must not lose sight of the equally instructive Pauline teaching on the body as one organism. Each part has its distinctive function. Yet no part works in isolation. One enables the other to perform its function. None is self-sufficient. The whole body of Christ, all God's people, then, can and must be involved in the theological task.

The tension between exclusive specialization and the free-for-all generalization need not be solved by rejecting one in favour of the other. (In many of the new nations, it has been quickly realized that rash dethronement of one class brings confusion, lack of direction and eventual failure.) A better solution is that of interlocking cooperation. The ordinary practitioners or believers can make a contribution to the theological enterprise. Such contribution can be made in one of two ways.

1. They can freely express their experience and understanding of God and Christ. The professional theologian will take over and systematize it. This resource material can be obtained in a variety of contexts. In Ghana, for instance, three very fruitful forums will be: (a) The testimony time during worship or at the prayer meeting when people share what the Lord has done for them; these may range from Christ coming into their life and saving them from hell to God healing their sick dog! (b) The content of prayer itself which reveals people's understanding of God as they express their expectations of what God should do, or as they ascribe worth to God. (In traditional society the libation prayers to the gods and ancestral spirits are a good source of the "theologies" of the pre-literate religions.) (c) The contributions made in discussion at Bible study also provide rich material for doing theology.

To harness these, the professional theologian must go to and learn from the people and do his or her theology *with* the people.

2. The second way in which ordinary believers can be involved in theology is to enable them to do theology themselves. This means that they must be given basic theological education. This must be given, not in a seminary or theological college, but right in their own everyday environment. Some form of informal theological education (e.g. theological education by extension) is called for. The programme must be such that the candidates' worldview, thought patterns, concepts and cultural outlook are not too seriously disturbed. In Africa, for example, the type of formal education we receive effectively alienates us from our own setting. Consequently many a brilliant African theologian is unable to relate to his or her people, to communicate the gospel effectively to them, or to understand their "crude" thoughts and statements about God.

Equipping the ordinary faithful to engage in theology will include making them aware of the challenges of ideologies and beliefs that contradict the Christian faith. They are to be encouraged to respond with dogma and practice. They must work out ways of combatting and forestalling ideological challenges.

The perspective for theology today
There have been loud calls for theology today to be a theology of the poor by which is meant that theology must deal with the situation of the

"poor and marginalized". This invariably means some kind of liberation theology. It cannot be doubted that theologians have a duty to address the issues of poverty, injustice, oppression, and other conditions that deny people the opportunity to realize themselves as made in the image of God.

However, this stance has a number of dangers. For one thing, it makes it look as if the theologian can invent his or her own "gospel", a message that only seeks the material welfare of the "poor" and glosses over their need to encounter Jesus of Nazareth. The theologian is an interpreter of the gospel—the faith once delivered by the apostles—and an articulator of the faith community's experience of God. Theologians only expound the seminal message already delivered. They cannot proclaim a new gospel.

Secondly, it suggests an almost exclusive emphasis on the antagonisms that Jesus Christ has already destroyed: "So there is no difference between Jews and Gentiles, between slaves and free men, between men and women; you are all one in union with Christ Jesus" (Gal. 3:28). Any theology that reintroduces conflicts among people is not good theology; theology must confront all the people with the challenge of Christ. It must equally proclaim good news to all the people. All this is to say that there must be a proper balance between presenting the message and challenge of Christ to redeem the human person as such — whether that person be rich or poor, male or female, oppressed or oppressor — and demanding a response for social justice.

Both the rich and the poor stand in need of reconciliation with God. There is also the whole complex issue of identifying the poor. In Ghana, for example, at the initial stages of the present "revolution" the poor were identified as the low-ranking workers, while the privileged were the managerial classes. Yet the so-called poor own more material wealth than the more educated so-called elite who live perpetually on borrowed money and have no houses of their own. On the other hand, the wealthy illiterate women traders who were maltreated for being rich are to be pitied for their ignorance and low level of living. Who, then, are the poor?

Another danger is that it is assumed that everywhere today the church's primary task must be political, racial and economic liberation. This is not the case. In some areas, such as West Africa, there is urgent need for developing an authentic African Christianity.

There is, again, the danger of confusing theology with prayers, witnessing, Christian service, Bible study, testimony. The issue of the role of "academic theology" — its task, opportunities and privileges in the university setting — must not be lost sight of.

New face for theology

Given that these various cautions are expressed and heeded, there should be much potential in the new emphasis. To do this theology, non-professional theologians are to be equipped and enabled to participate, while the professional theologians take their place among the ordinary people to do theology with them. The different levels of doing theology are to be recognized. These will include collecting and systematizing the variety of experiences, and understanding God's action in history. Sources for material will include prayers, testimonies, sermons. This new conscious and deliberate widening of the theological task need not displace the academic or professional theologians who are nevertheless called to be concerned with relevant issues of life in today's world, while not forgetting the fundamental task of stating and interpreting the call of God in Christ to be reconciled to live in such peace and harmony with their neighbours as will facilitate the realization of God's kingdom on earth. The new approach will involve institutions as well. Theological institutions will have to make theology more interdisciplinary and life-centred, making more use, for example, of the case study method in teaching theology. Churches will have to make Bible study more centred in life-issues than just theoretical learning of "what the Bible says". Theology will then be an enterprise not just for or by the academic and professional theologian alone, nor by the people as understood in populist contemporary "revolutions". It will be *theology by the whole people of God*.

III

A Personal Perspective

Barbara Brown Zikmund

In our world today those who call themselves Christian represent an incredible diversity. No longer can Christians assume certain common traditions or theologies as a basis of their identity. The exposure to diversity also establishes new patterns of accountability. It calls many Christians to repentance because of past injustices. It challenges every Christian to consider the promise that we are all one in Jesus Christ.

In our response to this situation we seek to be as inclusive as possible. Increasingly, however, I feel that doing theology and sustaining Christian community by making sure everyone is represented has its limitations.

In much of Christian history we have been able to treat pluralism as a temporary issue. Evangelization, integration, assimiliation, and cooperation, it was argued, would eventually draw everyone to common understandings of the Christian faith. The new ethnic and national churches have come to reject this assumption. There is value in preserving our diversity. We expect to benefit from pluralism. Out of the emerging theologies of third world churches the whole Christian community can grow beyond its patriarchal and European cultural biases. The problem is, we do not know how to value and benefit from pluralism and keep the integrity and rootedness of our faith and our church.

A personal testimony

In my own life I see this dilemma very clearly. I am a white female in a mainline Protestant denomination in North America. When I joined an

---

● Barbara Brown Zikmund is a member of the United Church of Christ of the United States of America. She is currently dean of the Faculty, Pacific School of Religion, and vice-president of the Association of Theological Schools of the USA and Canada. She is a member of the PTE Commission.

urban Congregational church in the early 1950s, it was generally content with the status quo. Then, the concerns of black Americans intruded into that world. I embraced the integrationist cause. I worked to get a black family in my church. I appreciated the ways in which the religious experience of blacks challenged my faith. Gradually I came to believe that integrated churches were good.

Next I became conscious of the patriarchal bias of my church and the fact that women were not treated equally. I argued that special groups were needed to help women claim their authority and appropriate the full power of the gospel. I rejoiced in the gifts of women. I pressed for equity for women in the church.

In both cases I am grateful to those who pushed my church to make sure all were represented and heard. I came to believe that the church of Jesus Christ needed to allow blacks and women to claim their place in church and society, not just for their sake, but because the church could only be the church when that happened. Finally, I helped other groups and caucuses get their concerns and agendas before the church. It was only fair. I knew oppression as a woman and I believed that the church would be faithful only when all were included.

I still believe this. Living with pluralism is a calling of the church. Discipleship demands that we never let the sins of racism and sexism take our churches hostage, even when the process is painful and the price is dear. In my critique of the ways in which we have tried to do theology "for" the people, I do not forget the importance of experiences which celebrate and explore our God-given diversity.

Yet, in recent years I have come to believe that our representative approach to theology in a pluralistic world seriously impairs the capacity of God's people to do theology. I speak very personally here. Two things happened to me as my church tried to remain inclusive in its theological work. First, the system became so ponderous in its efforts to be inclusive that I became tired, if not paralyzed. I believed in diversity and representation, but the results were exhausting and not very creative. Excellence deteriorated into mediocrity. Speed and risk became impossible.

Secondly, I did not like what happened to me. Instead of being energized in situations where representatives of various "peoples" came together to serve the church in new ways on truly representative boards and committees, I felt isolated and uprooted. I was still a token. Only this time all of us were tokens. It was a new kind of tokenism, not the one or two representatives of marginal groups added to a situation controlled by a dominant group, but a fragmented collection of uprooted folk with little awareness of their common bonds. In these new settings no one group was dominant. We were a conglomerate. Each of us came with our home loyalties. And although most of us believed that we did not need to put down our brothers and sisters in order to have our uniqueness recognized, we often failed to find our common loyalties. It is exciting to experience the diversity of the body of Christ. In the long run, however, I do not believe that the church of Jesus Christ can find its theological centre in this way.

What is the way out?

As I reflect upon this situation I see three ways out: (1) We can accept diversity and deal with it by favouring the cultivation of homogeneous churches and denominations which "naturally" emerge around the world. (2) We can view Christian diversity and pluralism as a temporary stage while pressing to re-examine and reclaim the assimilation/integration ideal of "one faith". (3) We can look for some new way of understanding the theological task which preserves our commitment to justice and equity in a diverse world *and* build upon existing communities of strength to forge theologies by the people suitable to various settings.

It is easy to recognize that in particular cultures and contexts the church of Jesus Christ will attract "like-minded" persons. Individuals and families need to find their faith home. Such a "home", or homogeneous community, will enable Christians to nurture their faith and to share their witness in the world. The church growth movement accepts this thinking at the local level. National and cultural pride shapes homogeneous, regional and confessional ecclesiastical organizations around the world. By trying to be inclusive and ignoring the significant cultural differences that separate peoples into diverse Christian traditions, the church some-times limits its potential for growth and frustrates its members. It may be poor stewardship to spend so much energy dealing with community diversity.

Or, if the cultivation of homogeneous Christian churches seems irres-ponsible (it does to me), we can seek to retrieve the assimilation model. Maybe not a melting pot, but a community of Christians who share some basic commonality. We can try to name our oneness in Jesus Christ again in terms which transcend cultural particularities by drawing upon the common historical foundations of Christianity. The ecumenical work which invites Christians to find a common apostolic faith in the Nicene Creed is one example of this. Churches with strong confessional tradi-tions can dig deeper into the old creeds, confessions, and catechisms to update their capacity to bind together new ideas and peoples. Many people crave this and believe that we can find our oneness in Christ.

Theologically, I have problems with both of these approaches. The first presumes that oneness in Christ is upheld by going around our differences, not by working through them. It certainly would be easier. However, I believe that the claim of justice does not allow us to ignore those who are different from us. The second presumes that Christian theology for these times can be done deductively. If we can just find the key era or document from which we can draw out a common theology which we can all affirm, we can transcend our differences.

There needs to be some alternative which allows every people to do theology with all of its unique particularity... and keeps each Christian mindful of the unity we share in Christ's death and resurrection. We need to develop a new way of defining and undertaking the theological task which uses context constructively and recognizes its limits.

For me this involves several things. Admitting that creative lively theology is happening in the church and setting out to find it. Living with the diversity discovered while seeking patterns of unity in all. Trusting that authentic theological reflection can be done inductively, rather than deductively. And drawing upon existing communities of natural theological discourse to do the work, while recognizing that no single community has an inclusive understanding of the faith.

"Uncertainty principle" in theological task

In modern science there is what is called the "uncertainty principle" or the "theory of indeterminancy". Nuclear scientists recognize that the sub-atomic world can never be known without distortion. This is because the very instruments and processes used to study particles intrude upon reality to such an extent as to change the results. In social science everyone knows that the way a question is phrased by an interviewer can influence the answer. In many areas of research, if the researcher removes something from an environment to study it, two things happen: the original context is no longer completely natural and the item removed may function differently in the isolation of the laboratory.

All of this is to say that the theological task involves an "uncertainty principle". Over the last few years I have been asked to serve on several ecumenical consultations to deal with theological concerns. They were wonderful experiences. I met many good people. I learned a great deal. But I also learned that theological reflection done in those carefully selected representative groups will always be inadequate. Even when each of us gave the project our best, we could never *be* at our best. This is because each of us functioned in token isolation from the natural communities of faith from which we came. We worked as an artificial conglomerate. The longer we worked together the more untrustworthy our work became. I am now convinced that theological integrity cannot be achieved in three-day meetings at conference centres far from home. I do not trust my own capacity to stay in touch with my theological roots when I am uprooted.

In earlier times it was possible to bring together certain elites with common traditions and presuppositions to theologize. Today the global context of Christianity makes this impossible. Either the theology will be insensitive to the realities of Christian life in different places, or it will be shallow. So what are we to do?

A theology by the people means that the Christian leaders of the world need to seek out those places where there is already great theological vitality and find new ways to share that without distorting its integrity. We need to discover and press existing natural communities of faithfulness which are not self-conscious to reflect theologically upon their life together, and to share that theology. We need to honour the historical traditions which have nourished these groups. Only after we have tapped the varieties of communal theological expressions already alive in our churches will we be able to forge an inclusive theology for the Christian peoples of the world.

In the meantime, ecumenical gatherings of "representatives" from varieties of churches need to restrain themselves. A theology by the people cannot be done by ecumenical gatherings of individuals uprooted from their natural communities of theological discourse. To use an analogy from political theory, a truly global Christian theology will emerge through federal alliances, rather than representative democratic structures. Theology by the people will flow upward from vital local centres. Through the Holy Spirit we will find new ways to claim what all these theologies have in common.

IV
Biblical Theology
Together with the People

Milton Schwantes

"Theology together with the people" *is not a recent theme.* For one thing, it is a profoundly biblical theme. The category of the people of God is present in the Old Testament. It is in the promise given to Abraham: "I will make of you a great nation" (Gen. 12:2). In their resistance to Pharaoh's oppression, this people structures and arms itself (Ex. 1ff.; 13:18). This people of the "corvéia" is part of Yahweh, "part of his heritage" (Deut. 32:9). The "formula of belonging", so vital to Old Testament theology, refers to it: "and I will take you for my people and I will be your God" (Ex. 6:7). The prophets give the category new meanings: from the darkness of the oppressive monarchy to the clarity of liberating justice for the poor (see Isa. 6:1-9:6 and 11:1-5).

One could try to explain this as a peculiarity of the Old Testament. After all, this literature came out of a context in which theology had a national and ethnic orientation. But the category of "people" is not abandoned in the New Testament. True, it assumes new characteristics. *Ethnos* no longer has the function (Matt. 3:9) that was attributed to it in the centuries previous to the Nazarene. But, precisely in this marvellous broadening of the horizons of the new people, the New Testament rescues dimensions which were developed in the Old Testament (review, for example, Gen. 17:4-6,16; Isa. 49:6, etc.), where Yahweh was known by other tribes before being worshipped as the God of Israel (Ex. 3:18; Judg. 5; in fourteenth-century Egyptian texts, there are certainly references to "Yahwehism"). In any case, the category of "people" continues to have a privileged place in the New Testament. Jesus is born in the midst of his people (Matt. 15:24, cf. Rom. 9-11). The apostle Paul in certain signifi-

---

● Milton Schwantes is on the staff of the Igreja Evangélica de Confissão Luterana no Brazil (the Evangelical Church of the Lutheran Confession in Brazil), Sao Leopoldo.

cant texts designates Christians as people of God (Rom. 9:24-26). In the letter to the Hebrews this category becomes important (Heb. 4:9). Condensed in 1 Peter 2:9-10 is a complete theology of the people of God. Indeed "the concept of 'people of God' is the oldest and most fundamental for defining the way the Church understands itself".[1]

Let's keep these comments in mind, to remind us of the biblical origin of our theme and perspective. However, in talking about it in our day, we do not immediately make the biblical connections. We link it instead to the issue of democracy. In the concept of "people" we are evoking a real power. We as Latin Americans are seeking to be people in whom popular power is constituted and established as collective will. In our history anti-people institutions have prevailed. Colonialist minorities, enslavers and capitalists imposed themselves, and continue to assert themselves against the indigenous people, against the slaves deported here, against immigrants, in short against popular will. Latin American history was made and written against the people. There was no lack of heroic resistance. There are significant stories. But today, certainly, the movements for the introduction of popular and democratic power are growing. The victorious revolutions in Cuba (1959) and Nicaragua (1979) were decisive events. Therefore, "theology together with the people" has revolutionary contours for us. The "theology of revolution" has not lost its relevance. In the words of Daniel Ortega, "Nicaragua is the Latin American issue."

In the light of the growth of popular power in our continent, in my opinion, two new aspects need to be added to what we have noted with respect to the category of people of God in the Bible.

In the Bible, the "people of God" is articulated as both tribes and clans. One of the Old Testament terms for people (*am*) even has "clan"/ "relations" as its first meaning. Israel is constituted as a group of tribes (Gen. 28ff.; Ex. 1ff.). It imposes itself over the kings of Canaan as a tribal union (see Joshua and Judges). Tribes and clans resist the oppression of the monarchy. In exile, tribalism is again proposed as a vital form of organization (Isa. 49:5f.). This theme recurs in the 12 disciples of Jesus. Tribalism includes mutual help between clans. It is an experience of the complementing of family needs, of the complementing of differences. In effect, tribalism is a distribution system. It represents the internal organic and dynamic character of the people of God, in particular of its peasant sectors. That is to say, in dealing with the people of God we cannot forget its most dynamic forms of organization, which were the

---

[1] H. Kung, *The Church*, London, Burns & Oates, Ltd., 1968.

clan and the tribe. This is relevant in order to sharpen our understanding of today's popular organizations.

It is important for us to perceive that in key moments the scriptures made extremely concrete their concept of the people of God. The new-born people of God from Sarah and Abraham and their descendants situate themselves on the periphery of the city-states of Canaan. The Israel that is organized in Egypt is a Hebrew "corvéia". The freed slaves that take the land of the kings of Canaan are landless Hebrews. In the prophets, the meaning of the people of Yahweh is in the poor and the impoverished, as is seen in Amos. In Micah, "the people" (2:1-5, 8-9; 3:1-4) are the poor peasants. In Isaiah, "the people" are seen precisely in the "face of the poor" (3:14-15). Jesus was sent "to the lost sheep of the house of Israel" (Matt. 15:24); the revelation becomes clear "to babes" (Matt. 11:25). The gospel is preached to the poor (Luke 4:16ff.). God "chose what is weak" (1 Cor. 1:27). In these and many other passages, the people of God is constituted starting with the poor. Impoverished women and men are not one fragment of the people, beside which exist others similar to them. The "people of Yahweh" is condensed into the poor, the church of Jesus. Nobody is excluded by this. But the centre around which the whole subsists is the poor.

Therefore, a "biblical theology by the people" must explain its hermeneutic mediations. What does it understand the people to be? We in this continent experience people as the popular and democratic power gradually consolidating itself against the systematic and secular usurpation of it through the years. In the light of such mediations, the concept of the people of God is narrowed down to the oppression and resistance of impoverished women and men. This resistance manifested itself in biblical times in tribal and clan models.

Decisive impulses of the new Latin American church

In the transformation of the concepts of "people", organization is fundamental. Without an organized people, there will be neither access to the land by those who work it, nor control of the factories by those who produce the goods. Those in power do not give an inch unless it is won by the organization of the people. The *popular movements* are vital, both as the seeds of a new society and as organizations that struggle for the imposition and advancement of popular interests. By popular movements I refer to the whole range of organizations that the popular classes create to express their most immediate demands and their struggles for power, to give viability to their survival and to advance in their social efforts. I think, for example, of our indigenous people in their struggle for land and to recover their own culture, of the workers and their unions, of the neighbourhood and street organizations, of the mothers' clubs, of the peasant unions. This true organizing source of the popular classes exercises and foments popular power, the people.

Decisive impulses for the new Latin American church, for liberation theology and for a re-reading of the Bible are the result of conscious and consistent insertion of the church in the popular movements. In the "option for the poor", the concept of "poor" is not something undefined or amorphous, or an abstraction. The option for the poor does not deal with a concept of "poor" but rather with the organized reality of the poor. The option for the poor is an option for its organization. It brings the churches into the popular movements!

From that point on come other tasks for the churches. We are not accustomed to being in close proximity with the popular movements. For centuries our churches had been almost insensitive to the people's afflictions, largely indifferent to the cries of the "warehouses of human-ity", because the churches were themselves within the circles of the powerful. Let's look at the way our ecclesiastical organizations are. Theoretically we hold the idea that all those who are baptized have access to decision-making. This in theory makes for democracy. But this internal church democracy is very restrictive in practice. Generally speaking, it is filtered through so many selective processes and representative channels that the people remain excluded. There are very few cases where popular power has access to the decision-making organisms of the churches. The church structure has been marked by feudal authoritarianism and mana-gerial centralism, which do not take sufficiently seriously the baptized people. Therefore, openness to the popular movements calls for a new ecclesiogenesis in which the Holy Spirit reinvents the church.

The new Latin American reading of the Bible has its roots in this process, by which churches and Christians are in solidarity with workers and peasants in their struggle for liberation, and in which those same impoverished people make up the church. I want to emphasize this rediscovery of the Bible.

For us, a "theology together with the people" must be in solidarity with the Latin American people, secularly exploited and removed from the power that is exercised against them on the one hand and with the liberating experiences that make evident the possibility of triumphing over the powers of extortion on the other. In this sense, a "theology by the people" needs to clarify its historic mediations, among which *inter alia* are the popular movements. For us, "theology together with the people" has a specific context that affects our theologizing and in relation to which we theologize. Such interaction, obviously, need not discard theology and the scriptures.

A *new reading of the Bible* is shaking our continent: a *people's reading*. It seems to us that the years to come will place this reading more and more in the centre of the confrontations. While the new reading appeared as a "defenceless flower", or as a "light breeze" (C. Meesters), today turbulence is on the horizon. With the Bible becoming once again the great teacher for the people's communities, it carries the symbols for liberation. This usage of the Bible is being questioned, with more and more vigour, by the ecclesiastical elite. We are yet in the preliminary stages of this conflict around biblical hermeneutics.

Characteristics of re-reading the Bible together with the people

It does not come from academics. We can discard academics. For the academic exegetes, for all their meticulous labour, were not sufficiently sensitive to determined world visions. Nor was their work born out of a structuralist or materialist or historicist frame of reference even if these and other points of view can help in the assessment of the new phenomenon. The new biblical reading was born in the pastoral ministry of small church groups. It comes from the practice of faith, from resistance and the organization of the poor.

We, the agents of pastoral ministry, were sensitized by the social issues, particularly the tremendous misery all around. We saw how the poor were increasingly becoming alienated from the church. Our preaching and our rituals fell on deaf ears. So we began to listen, to consult and to learn along with the popular movements. Exposing ourselves to the way the poor did hermeneutics we were brought to new vistas. New doors were opened. The consultation of the people in community is, then, the birthplace of the new reading. It is the constant matrix. The popular community is the source of the new reading of the Bible. This means that it is not exactly new, nor is it exactly a re-reading. Actually, it is another reading. It is the reading of the poor.

The people discover their face. The effects of pastoral work can be formulated in these terms: people are not spectators of rituals but rather practitioners of their faith in organizational forms. In their experience in church groups, the people give evidence and flesh to their words. They go on to sharpen their eyes' perceptions and to filter information. They exercise their action on the world around them. They learn in their social practice. They have confidence in their decisions. They go into resistance. They sing: "We are new people."

In the current Latin American situation it is important that this communitarian and personal experience of having a face and of being somebody is encouraged by the pastoral ministry of the church. The experience helps them to reach out to persons who otherwise would have difficulty in adhering to the liberation process. In many sectors of our continent, the pastoral ministry, an apprentice of the popular movements, became its indispensable supporter and ally.

The Bible contributed considerably to this discovery of having a face, of being people. A peasant, upon perceiving that God created the first people just like peasants, gets confirmed in his need to defend his possession. A woman who listens to Deborah grows in her willingness to face up to the authorities. The poor, in country and city, join forces when they realize that God acted through the exploited Hebrews and the Nazarene peasant movement, people who were poor to the point of having no place to go to.

Therefore, "biblical theology together with the people" is rooted in the conviction that the Bible as used in people's movements helps give people a face and dignity. The biblical experience is translated into the experience of the citizens. By reappropriating the scriptures, the communities of the poor reappropriate their right to life.

"Spiritualizing" of scripture in churches

The interpretation of the scripture must be spiritual, in the sense of invoking the Spirit with fear and trembling. Thus we do not criticize a hermeneutic for being spiritual. But the problem lies in what is understood as spiritual. In church circles, the spiritual usually tends to be separated from earthly things, an attitude which assumes that undefinable atmosphere of the religious. In spite of all that, in such spiritual sublimations these earthly things are covered with a language that is so ethereal and general that they lose their concrete reference. They remain restricted to the religious department.

The reading of the Bible carried out in popular communities is also *spiritual* in a very intense way. The suspicion that in the practices of the popular church spirituality is not exercised is not true to the facts. The spiritual interpretation appears in another form in these communities. I would risk formulating it in the following terms: in them spirituality explicitly incorporates what is concrete about life. It is mixed with their cries as well as their personal and collective successes. The measure of what is spiritual is not only the religious drama, but also the drama of hunger and of manual work. Strikes and land invasions, a new bus stop or day care centre are integrated into spirituality with the same intensity as the sermon and the sacraments.

For these reasons, a "biblical theology together with the people" will be eminently spiritual, but it will be so in a very incarnate and historical way. The mediation of biblical spirituality is above all its reality of alienated work and its utopia of free work.

Presence in the struggles of life

The Bible is *presence in the struggles of life*. A peasant typically expresses it thus: "In the day-to-day struggle we see that the Bible is our best companion." In their action with the people, the biblical story appears as something real today. The biblical characters take on current meanings. Our own organizational experiences, with their advances and setbacks, are rediscovered in the texts. In today's struggles for land, the biblical scene reappears. The revolutionary victories are models of Easter, in the words of Molina. In short, the scripture is a presence which illuminates our conflicts. What a contrast to academic biblical studies where the formulation of the good news is almost irrecoverably determined by the cultural limits of their time, creating a deep abyss between us and the Bible!

Academics are naturally suspicious of fundamentalism, concordance oversimplification and lack of critical distance. But such critical voices generally approach the scripture from a cultural perspective and from the experience of the so-called consumer "modern man". Our approach does not give priority to such mediations. The popular communities tune in to the scriptural content from a concrete and material perspective and from a practice of struggle and conflict. At this level, the Bible is a book for today. From the cross and martyrdom our history of yesterday and today is planted! It is Calvary! The Hebrews in conflict over land is our day-to-day struggle!

This sense of the presence of the Bible also knows how to maintain its critical distance from the biblical content. For example, when the community reads the part of Romans 13 about subjection to the authorities, people immediately see its incompleteness because the prophets opposed the kings, and realize that Revelation talks about it a different way (Rev. 13). Or again, the Pauline injunction that "the women should keep silence in the churches" (1 Cor. 14:33-36) immediately evokes general protest. Effectively, a reading of the scripture that holds the Bible as "the best companion in the day-to-day struggle" does not leave out a critical viewpoint.

Therefore, for us a "biblical theology together with the people" gives primacy to the experience of the closeness of the Bible. The scriptures are present in the conflicts that lead to freedom.

Prophetic reading

A popular reading is a prophetic reading; it emphasizes, in the Bible, *the denouncing and the announcing*. Gustavo Gutierrez significantly has a chapter on "Solidarity and Protest" in his book *Liberation Theology*. The popular communities see the Bible simultaneously as denouncing poverty as injustice and announcing that in the solidarity of the poor and with the poor new hope is born.

The biblical re-reading in Latin America began with denouncing the secular misery to which our people are subjected. In a context of hunger, unemployment, eviction from the land and genocide, the biblical content supported those who denounced misery as the fruit of wealth. "I have seen the affliction of my people... and have heard their cry" (Ex. 3:7) came into its own. In the popular communities, the Bible is experienced as articulating and broadening the prophetic denunciation.

Denunciation by itself is tiring and only looks back at what was opening up wounds. It needs the balance of the announcement, of the prolepsis of what is to come. The advances achieved by the popular movements and the revolutionary organizations give hints that hope is viable. The scripture is marvellous in its eschatological colouring! "They shall beat their swords into ploughshares... they shall sit each one under his vine" (Mic.4:3-4).

Of course the denunciation and announcement have always been cultivated in church circles. But the church's insistence on explaining everything in terms of the moral and the personal cannot be sufficient basis for deducing the social aspects. Collective misery and hope are not merely projections of personal will. The dynamics are different. Both are relevant, but they do not, however, follow linearly; rather, they are dialectically juxtaposed.

So, a "biblical theology together with the people" will emphasize the scripture as untiring denunciation of poverty and as inexhaustible announcement of social distribution. A hermeneutic that does not include such ideas will be neither biblical nor in the interests of the people.

It is important that poor people are the agents of interpretation. Suffering women and deprived men in community take the meanings of the Bible as their own. They tune in to its content. They do it like experts. Such reading goes straight to the central point of the Bible, namely the Christ of the Gospels. He is born poor and persecuted. He lives with the marginalized: women, children, sick, hungry. He died on the cross for us, and he lives. In this story the social conflict is clarified: the dominant keep up a fierce struggle against the poor and their project. In spite of everything, it is viable to transcend the social struggle.

Further, such reading goes to another central point of the Bible in pointing out the liberation of the Hebrews who were deprived of all they possessed because of the interests of the Pharaoh. The Latin American communities were not the ones who discovered the centrality of the Exodus. Here consciousnesses were deepened: God enters into history on the side of the weak.

Therefore, a "biblical theology together with the people" recognizes that the interpreters, the preferred hermeneutic agents, are in the popular communities. Wouldn't this be hasty? That is our next point.

The peasant experience

In the preceding sections we concentrated on the biblical concept of the people of God in the poor. We also saw that reading through the eyes of the poor is an entry into biblical hermeneutics. The communities of the poor take on, then, the role of qualified *hermeneutic agents*. J.S. Croatto expresses this very well in his latest book: "The poor and oppressed possess the most adequate 'claim' to re-read the kerygma of the Bible."[2] What are the implications of the claim?

Let us approach this issue from the specific stance of the peasants, one of the most dynamic sectors of the popular movement, and in light of the peasant experience that "in the day-to-day struggle we see that the Bible is our best companion". Because peasants live nature's cycle so intensely and religiously, the farmer can take on the eminently religious language of the sacred texts. Rural people perceive the Bible as a "companion" not primarily because the texts are in religious language, but rather because they speak of the struggle for land.

One could attribute this closeness of the Bible to cultural similarity. Because it speaks about the uses and customs of the desert, the peasant could feel attracted by the biblical narratives. For the farmers, the Bible is vibrant not only because it deals with rural customs, but also because it reveals to them the "day-to-day struggle".

---

[2] *Hermenéutica Bíblica* (Biblical Hermeneutics), Buenos Aires, La Aurora, 1984, p.69.

It is not enough to attribute their attraction for the Bible to the religious or rural language contained in the texts. The language is influential but not decisive. What is decisive to the experience of proximity is the scriptures' content and its position with respect to the peasants' ownership of the land and the collective use of its fruits.

Because of this, a "biblical theology together with the people" will have to work with the hermeneutic meaning of biblical reading from the perspective of the poor, in the sense of making explicit the basic communities' role as hermeneutic agents.

Until now our emphasis has been hermeneutic; our focus was the interpretative process in the midst of a transforming practice. A "theology together with the people", before all else, must be a hermeneutic exercise.

Now I would like to direct our attention to a more historical perspective. What is the correlation between the *scriptures and poor people*? Is the scripture a text that speaks about suffering people? Or could it even be a text that originates in the poor? These are questions which require historical investigation and arguments. In our society and churches these tasks are delegated to pastors and theologians. Several study groups are dedicated to clarifying these issues.

There is a tendency to dismiss as inadequate those explanations of the origins of the biblical text which are deduced from the personality or temperament of its author. Nor is there much sympathy for seeing the origin of the scriptures in the city-dwellers and dominant sectors. Others would even deny that the search for textual origins has any significance.

For myself I incline to the side of those who try to demonstrate the possibility that the scriptures, historically, are popular literature, i.e. the texts are the fruit and product of the peasantry, especially of the poor peasants. Significant arguments can be developed to support this hypothesis. Let us look at some.

The relevant contents of the scriptures do not effectively originate in the city, nor do they correspond to the interests of the dominant sectors. This is so clear that a meticulous detailing is unnecessary. Jesus came from the peasants and acts among them, especially together with the most poor, the women and children. He is sentenced as a peasant who puts the temple or empire into danger. His followers endangered the economy of the temple. His thesis that the temple was a house of prayer was contrary to the understanding of this institution as it was then set up. In the Old Testament, the liberation of the Hebrews is one of the preferred traditions of the rural people. It is their creed! The force of the Abrahamic minorities, of the prophetic movements and of ancient wisdom breathes new winds from the popular and peasant movements. There are many indications that support the possibility that the scriptures were born in the periphery. That does not mean that every verse or certain parts were not produced by other social sectors. Paul's letters were written by a Roman citizen who had access to education. But even this author of such profound letters is no more than an interpreter of a peasant movement: the death and resurrection of Jesus of Nazareth.

The form of scriptures also indicates outlines of popular literature. If it were urban literature of the dominant sectors, literature conceived as a whole, it should inevitably have a more organic character. We would expect it to be a more continuous text. But that's not the case. Its scenes are brief. Its texts are, for the most part, short and complete in themselves. The major part of the Bible is, in fact, a compilation of these smaller texts. The scriptures are a collection of episodes. This gives it precisely the framework and the form of popular literature. The first groupings of stories did not even occur at the hands of the collectors of larger literary units, like, for example, the gospels. These groupings still have the mark of the popular form of collecting stories and grouping episodes: they bring together a few episodes, generally three or five, like for example in Mark 4 or Amos 1-2.

But the peasants were illiterates who could neither read nor write. This, however, need not constitute an objection to treating the scriptures as popular literature. After all, a story's birth is in the tradition, in telling and retelling. In this process of memorization the scene acquires cohesion. The writing does not make the story: memory fixes it. One of the preferred places for the circulation of memory was in worship, in the celebrations in villages and families. Meanwhile there were other popular centres for the settling of the historical memory, for example the house, the doorway, the prophetic circles, the popular army, the Christian communities.

But would it be possible to attribute so much creativity to the culture and religion of the peasant people? It is difficult to admit the possibility that the scriptures had their birth among the impoverished, if we think about the social conditions that operate in capitalism or in slavery, for example. Under those circumstances the popular culture suffers constant bombardment by the dominant interests. However, even in such unfavourable conditions there is cultural-popular resistance. This was even more evident in the socio-economic conditions of the biblical world! The relations of that time were marked by their tributarian aspect. We know that in tributarian societies the peasantry retained significant space under their own control. The peasants of the Bible had control of their parcel of land. Access to the land was controlled by the clan rather than by the state. In this context, it is perfectly reasonable to suppose that the villages had their own religious expression. It seems to me that the scriptures are memory elaborated in the free spaces of the peasants and villages.

For these reasons, there are solid arguments for postulating the thesis that the scriptures are popular and peasant literature, especially promoted by the most impoverished sectors. For a "biblical theology together with the people", this possibility has special pastoral relevance.

I am not in a position to propose conclusions and implications, because I recognize that a great many aspects and details are not sufficiently developed in these preliminary notes. Let me merely summarize what I have tried to do in this paper:

— The people of God is constituted, in the flesh, in the poor and crucified.
— The new Latin American reading of the Bible has its birth in the listening and in the service of the churches together with the popular movements.
— The new reading of the Bible is rooted in pastoral ministry.
— "In the day-to-day struggle we see that the Bible is our best companion."
— The poor Christian communities are privileged hermeneutics agents.
— The Bible is possibly popular literature, arising from the peasants of Palestinian tributarianism.

V
Theology at the Base

Ian M. Fraser

The assignment given me includes the request that I offer some insight into people's theology in Europe. I could fulfill my task by quoting extensively from documents — "markers" which basic Christian communities put down to register the stage they have reached. But I do not think that kind of material offers a lively enough indicator of the kind of theology these small communities are creating in Europe.

A second approach would be to study effects. How would we know whether people had been doing their biblical and theological work in Holland some years ago, when illegal immigrants were being hunted down? The immigrants were taken into the homes of members of basic Christian communities, sheltered, protected from the authorities and found work. In such action lies the evidence that Dutch basic Christian communities had been doing their theology. Other members of basic Christian communities got their heads broken by the police at Comiso, where nuclear missiles are being installed in Sicily — the fact that they were there showed they had done their theology. To be the genuine article theology has to be put to work to change history.

A third approach could relate to processes and methods. We could look at the way in which, over a period, people have wrestled with the scriptures in the Holy Spirit, seeking to make real and deep the approach to the Bible and to life.

People, Bible, world in dynamic relationship
I choose a different entry point: how the Bible has been used to domesticate and subdue peoples, and how the people are recovering their freedom.

● Ian Fraser is a research consultant to the Scottish Churches Council's Basic Communities Project, previously called the Shalom Project.

In several parts of Latin America I was assured by church members that they had been brought up to believe that if they read the Bible directly they would go off their heads. A party from Britain visiting Italian basic Christian communities in May 1984 were told that, up till Vatican II, Italians were forbidden to read the Bible individually or in groups. A priest had to be in control when the Bible was consulted; only safely filtered through his mind could its message be received. This use of the Bible to domesticate Christians has now been unmasked. A community near Zwolle in Holland provided the following reflection:

> Every time we go to the Bible we have to reckon with a thick layer over it of traditional and ideologically slanted interpretations. Here is one instance to illustrate how our own basic Christian community got over that hurdle. It concerns the widow who put her last coins into the treasury of the temple. Traditionally she is supposed to have acted well. Traditionally Jesus' words were of praise for her. We looked more closely at this text. We came to believe that Jesus is condemning the clergy of his day for confusing a woman like this so that she gives the little money she has to robbers who demean the worship. Jesus is angry that people can be taken in by religious manipulators.

Ciro Castaldo, member of a community in Naples, who is also technical secretary for the Italian basic Christian communities, included the following reflection in an interview:

> The fundamental thing for the groups is the reappropriation of the word of God. The Bible has to be read by the people of God in the light of the historical experience which is a present reality for them. This makes Bible reading a very concrete activity! The expert, the professional theologian, has a place *within* communities acting thus. The expert has to be one who has shared in the community as it seeks to live the faith. In such a living context, and there alone, the historical-critical knowledge of the text provides an important contribution. Let me repeat — the place of the Bible is absolutely fundamental in the life of the basic Christian communities.

The first point I make then is that the Bible has been used to domesticate believers. That attempt has failed. The basis for doing theology is going into the hands of the people themselves.

My second point follows. In the traditional use of the Bible, creation has often been devalued and separated from salvation. Creation, all that makes up life as we face it today, is God's concrete gift and work. It provides the only available terms in which to express obedience. Creation must be given full attention if we are going to be serious about what God is doing in the world and our response to that world. The terms for the obedience of Christians in the world include analysis and research — a variety of ways of taking stock of reality. Remember what is said in St John's Gospel — we are born not of the will of the flesh nor of the will of man but of God. We *are* born of the will of flesh. We *are* born of the will of man. What does it mean, then, this emphasis on our being born of God? It is surely a reminder that, not haphazardly but of God's choice, we are born into a particular piece of history and located in particular places — what we have to offer God at the end of our lives must be the obedience appropriate to that time and those places. For those born of God contemplation must find a new significance and place. Contemplation is not going out of gear behind green fields. It is a form of dynamic availability in which one remains attentive and teachable before what God presents us with in the world, including its mystery, during that particular slice of history entrusted to us for our obedience as persons in community.

We must take account of the fact that our own assignment will come within God's liberating love for all humankind. So we also need to identify associates "out there" with whom to labour in the work of the kingdom. The following quote comes from another interview with a member of a Dutch basic Christian community:

Question: Why did this basic community come into being?
Answer: The official churches are dominated by people with middle-class interests and ways of thinking. They refuse serious engagement in political, social and economic matters, refuse to take sides against oppression and on behalf of the poor and of those made voiceless in our society. Solidarity of the kind we showed was called "communistic", "socialistic", "left-wing".
Question: But are not the basic communities made up of middle-class people?
Answer: That's true. But we recognize our middle-class character, and try to analyze our class position and bend it to the service of oppressed people.
Question: Are you working with marginalized people, making community with them?
Answer: There has to be solidarity, not just words: but solidarity of the kind which *they* want, which *they* define.
Question: Are there new bridges across the class divides?
Answer: Understanding may grow; but we cannot become one of them — we can take sides; but we must do so recognizing that it is their fight, not ours.
Question: So your work is (a) to back them up and (b) get middle-class people to see things their way?
Answer: Two steps are required. One is the analysis of our own middle-class position. Only then is it possible to be a disturbing force among our own class — that is the second step.

So both the Bible with its challenges and the world with its struggles are to be taken seriously.

My third point is that this can only be done by those who accept the risks of living. The Bible has been used to produce well-instructed paralytics, people who set out to know more and more about the text and have no intention of doing one single thing about it. Many house groups and many Bible study groups are of that kind. They cannot be part of the Hebrew/Christian tradition which insists that you cannot know God and God's purposes unless you spend life first *following the light you see* and only then seeking more light.

Twelve years ago I was in Rome with basic Christian communities at one of the city-wide gatherings which they hold twice a year. These, overwhelmingly Roman Catholic in membership, were being led in Bible study by a Baptist minister and his people. I met the Baptist minister afterwards and said to him: "How did this kind of thing come about?" He answered: "This way. We Baptists believed that everything that mattered was in the Bible. So we dug into the Bible, and dug into the Bible. As time went on, it became very clear to us we were making no impact at all on those around us, giving no Christian witness. Then we looked across and saw Roman Catholics who were making a real faith-impact on people in the neighbourhood. In spite of the history of dismissiveness and persecution which we had suffered at their hands, we just had enough grace to go across to them and say, 'We think you have found something about the faith which we need to find too.' They said, 'Join us.' Then in no time they were saying to us, 'But you know so much more about the Bible! We are ignoramuses. It is real partnership that we now have together in the gospel.'" "What has been the result?" I asked. He said: "You will find my people now where there is very sub-standard housing getting it upgraded and properly rehabilitated. You will find them going in delegations to the city council to push for housing for the homeless. You'll find them taking up housing policies on a national scale. Now the Bible really speaks to us!"

The first attempt of the Baptists was to make the Bible something in itself. That it never can be. The Bible has to be wrestled with in the Holy Spirit, by people facing the particular terms of that slice of history and geography which God has entrusted to them.

Open, disciplined reflection on liberating activity

There is now a widespread acknowledgment that the main theme of the Old Testament is the exodus from slavery in Egypt and the main theme of the New Testament is the exodus which Jesus accomplished in Jerusalem for all people. That is, the Bible has to be read with *a readiness to listen to the reality, nature and scope of God's liberating activity*; and those who read have to be ready to join in that enterprise. You will find among basic Christian communities a great conviction that that is the way in which the Bible has to be approached and wrestled with in the Holy Spirit. This quotation is from one of these communities:

> We are convinced that God is present in every situation where human liberation takes shape. The God of the scriptures is for all people and at the same time takes sides with the voiceless people, the oppressed people whom he leads to freedom. We believe that faith comes alive not only from the revelation and the dogmatic tradition of the church but in interplay between revelation and our experiences — very ordinary, normal experiences. There are three elements — the revelation (the story, the gospel, the tradition); political engagement; and what we find from that involvement and the analysis of society. It is these, in interplay, which make up believing faith. Theology grows out of their inter-relationships.

Theologizing implies more than reflection — it is disciplined reflection. In my own words: "The word 'theology' describes the disciplined attempts of human beings to understand how the world has been and is being affected by God's presence and activity within it; to make out what kind of God God is, and what is God's agenda. Christian theology proposes Jesus Christ as the unique focus for this search."

I want to emphasize only one part for the moment: "The word 'theology' describes the disciplined attempts of human beings..." Disciplined attempts to grapple with what the community has confronted, responded to and understood as it has tried to live the faith in the world are necessary for that to result in theology.

To do theology you need a community with different forms of involvement, different experiences and angles of insight: a community, variously gifted, which invests time and energy in uncovering the terms of situations faced and in searching the scriptures for light on them; which thus learns to live in the world under the discipline of the word attentive to the Spirit. The people of God is the only possible theological community.

The laos of God, this kingdom of priests, is a sinful people, a fallible people, a people who may do even the right thing at the wrong time because they do not give an adequate prayerful attentiveness to what God is asking at particular stages of history. Within the *laos* of God are theological specialists. They are often sinners more than others — with undiagnosed and unchallenged class, patriarchal, sexist, racist and other biases. They nonetheless represent elements of challenge and confirmation regarding the faith once delivered to the saints.

What is the gift God gives to humanity in its church? A community who have enough in Jesus Christ to take one another to task and challenge one another to the hilt *and still stay in fellowship.* The difference which should mark the Christian community from others is that in it the awkward questions are not avoided: people can push them as hard as they will go, and stay in fellowship with one another. Out of such honest and disciplined searching, theology may emerge.

Such a community was encountered in West Germany, the Tee-stubegemeinde in Wurzburg. I quote from an interview with members:

> When something has gone wrong with our relationships, we propose to deal with these matters honestly and openly with one another. This does not mean judging one another, as if one were superior to the other; but accepting one another in all our guilt, anxiety and weakness, just as Jesus had accepted us. (There is a desire to be) ... accepted by one another exactly as we are. We want to work at this so that we can make demands on one another and also criticize one another and still strengthen one another and stay together. (Once a year each person has to affirm adherence to "this general position", which makes openness and truth-telling an agreed part of a trusting fellowship.)

I draw attention to one particular element which Gea Boessenkool provided in an interview. Gea, who is one of the coordinators of the Dutch basic Christian communities, offers criticism which we need to hear.

> *Question:* What do you see to be the basis from which all this fresh thinking is coming? Is it biblical study? What is giving you fresh perspectives on old types of relationship?
> *Answer:* It is not easy to answer in general. I can answer for myself. For me it was my own experience as a woman in this world which I found coinciding with the experiences of other women in my environment. I have been encouraged by some stories in the Bible, from women. But, theologically speaking, we are in a state of poverty, because theologians have always been men, so that even the language in which we talk about the Bible is masculine language. We have very much to do to feminize this language and to use our own experiences when reading the Bible. The feminist theological courses in Holland are very few in number. All those who lead them have to fight to develop different approaches from those of their masculine colleagues. Because they have no tradition from which to handle their material it means they must go back to the very beginning, look for a new language, look for a new hermeneutic, look for other interpretations of Bible history!
> I have been encouraged, for example, by the story of Ruth and Naomi in the Old Testament, and also by some women's stories told about Jesus, e.g. the story of Jesus with the woman who was bent down and Jesus said to her:

"Daughter of Abraham, get up on your feet." I think that that is a very good story for women in our time too. He called her a daughter of Abraham, he set her on her feet as a member of the people of Israel, of the Jewish people, no longer as a woman outside society. I can imagine when someone like Jesus says such things to you you get on your feet and you walk tall! But afterwards it is very difficult not to bend down again.

We have to support each other! In my personal life it has been my experience that women can support each other very well. I have had some periods in my life which have been very difficult to get through, looking for hope from I do not know where. And then, from somewhere, women came around me to give support. There was also the basic Christian community movement — women in it were very important to me. I think that what tells is the strength women can draw on to support each other, to see the problems of one another without taking over responsibility for dealing with them (and without all that good advice that everyone always gives in such a case). I think that, in the feminist movement, we have learned to speak together, to support each other in society, but also in church and in reading the Bible. In all those places we have learned to support each other, to talk with each other, to listen to each other.

It is in Christian communities rather than in theological institutes that you find a breadth of critical judgment which helps to transform and rectify faith-experience so that it gains theological substance. Here is one product of such thinking. In Portugal, in a group in Oporto, this was said when we were considering the Virgin Mary and her place in the whole gospel: "Physical virginity is not of any significance in understanding Mary as virgin. What Mary was prepared for was to have a child who would not be her own. She was prepared to be available to God for whatever he wanted of her. That is the root of her virginity."

Springs down below

In such a community people can be free to do the truth and to fashion and refashion theology (theology always needs to be fashioned and refashioned). Next question — who can do this? One of the great discoveries of our time is that many people have recovered their own stories and their own histories and their own cultures from colonial domination. There are new sources for theology all over the world wherever this has happened. But even more important is the rejection of the idea that professors with ten degrees have some edge in doing theology over, say, illiterates. They realize that when it comes to knowing God and discerning the ways of God, illiterates can be at least as competent. When it comes to doing theology these two have different kinds of contributions to offer, no more than that.

We met a sister in Belgium who told us this story about her work in a place called Pueblo Joven in Brazil:

> There are very poor people there, there was no water, there was no light, it was terrible. We had to go there because the bishop did not want to renew the contract with us. One of the things which he said was: "You are not in the things which are holy." I told it to one of the women of Pueblo Joven and she was very angry. She said: "For the bishop what is holy is all that is happening inside the church. For me what is holy is the future of my people."

What the woman said to the nun showed she not only had better human perceptions, not only had better faith perceptions, but was theologically mature while the bishop was theologically illiterate. He was not talking about the way of holiness at all, he was talking about participation in sacralized routines. Being holy derivatively implies being set apart *from* and *for*. To be set apart *from* all other concerns *for* a future that God has for your people expresses the essence of holiness. It was the slum-dweller's words which had theological depth.

Here is one more example of such perceptiveness. At Guimaraes in Portugal when, in November 1984, we were meeting with a basic Christian community, a young girl was among the members. The communities in Portugal are poor in the sense that they are basic workers, sometimes unemployed — not like the Dutch ones, for instance, who are mainly middle-class. She said: "I have come to realize that when Jesus said I came not to bring peace but a sword he was telling the poor not to sit under oppression but to get up and fight." I very much doubt whether that biblical perception could have come from somebody doing Bible research in a study, in a middle-class situation.

We have to reckon with the fact that, whether it squares with our idea of justice or not, God has chosen the poor to provide the essential perspectives by which the church must live. Not all poor — for there are domesticated poor — but the poor who have taken their courage in both hands, gained dignity, and aspire to that abundance of life which Jesus Christ wants for them in face of a world which would deny it to them.

How are basic communities basic?

I have been asked what the word "basic" means when applied to Christian communities. I make four points.

For one thing, the word points to basic people, people at the bottom of the heap, people who have minimal resources and minimal status and who, but for God's declaration of their importance, would not know they have dignity and place in his world. On a world scale, the main membership of these communities comes from that category.

Secondly, "basic" applies to those who, instead of taking opportunities for upward mobility and promotion and whatever advantages they may gain for themselves, make a thrust of downward mobility to the base to be alongside those who are there. It is significant that the poor people we were with in the Philippines about two years ago recognized such middle-class people in Europe as partners in one struggle. Jesus was lower middle-class, let us say, as a carpenter, and he practised downward mobility to be alongside the outcasts. There lies a second element in the meaning of "basic".

A third element has to do with getting at the basics of the faith, clearing from its core the distortions and accretions that we have managed to add as churches.

And the fourth flavour of "basic" refers to building up the faith and the church from below, from the base. It means not taking from ecclesiastics "up there" what they have thought out and packaged for others. It means acting as adult Christians who take responsibility for living what they believe and working out the belief by which they live.

Parts to play in reinventing theology as the people's work

I distinguish three roles, but they are by no means the only ones.

1. One thing which stands in contrast to what happens in the normal life of the church is the place that children are given in basic Christian communities. Older people sit at their feet. That is the way Jesus said it should be. They take a full part in the praying and the preaching — small children, 7 to 8 years old! The people of God, then, the whole people comprising children, women and men are called to live the faith, to perceive the substance of what they are living, to articulate it and develop a critical understanding of what it means. They are the theological community.

But basic communities are even more marvellously gifted, in that they possess the languages which are proper for theology, which we the ordained most often do not — the language of the streets, the language which Jesus used. One thing which follows is that they hold a special responsibility to identify that theology which is latent in life-responses which have a kingdom character, especially when these come from people who make no Christian profession.

2. The second role is that of the theological specialist. The theological specialist is not meant to accompany the people in order to articulate and systematize the people's thinking. The specialist does not *own* the struggles of the people. It is for those who own the struggles to do the theology. The whole community is needed to discern what is essentially happening and what God is essentially saying in it. But the theological specialist has two very precious, I would call them indispensable, resources to contribute. One is textual and technical knowledge which is not accessible to most people, at least not at present (although there are basic Christian communities — I know of two, one has only 18 members, the other has only 6 — who have allocated members to learn Greek and Hebrew in order that they may have a scholarship resource within the small communities themselves). The other is the work of inserting others into the communion of saints. What I intend by the latter is that work which helps other Christians to see how faith has moved through history and where people are moving in faith to the ends of the earth today.

3. Third is the role of theological institutions and of people like myself — both in my previous work in Selly Oak Colleges and now as research consultant to the Scottish Churches Council. One urgent responsibility is to develop techniques designed to put theology back in people's hands and give them confidence in working out their own theology.

Another thing I think we need from institutes today is resources to combat contemporary ideologies and distortions of faith. I think particularly of the economic/military complexes which are among today's principalities and powers, and of the calling to unmask these, to oppose them, to help other people to see them in a true light and not worship their idols. Alongside these I would place the crusades of rich, self-confident fundamentalists who are servants of these complexes, who with their assertive campaigns are trying to ravish Latin America with Bible and gold as the conquistadores once did with Bible and sword.

VI

A Theology by Minjung

David Kwang-sun Suh

The bridegroom of Ahndong

Ahn-Gook was the good-looking son of Kim Sook, a renowned scholar and high-ranking government official. As soon as Ahn-Gook started to talk, his scholarly father began teaching him how to read. But the son could not identify even the most basic letters such as the sky and the earth, even after three months of learning. Thinking that his son was too young to learn, the father waited for several years. When he tried again, he employed every measure to press and encourage Ahn-Gook to learn. He even scolded and whipped him, but the result was the same as before. At the age of fourteen Ahn-Gook had still learned nothing. His father, in disappointment, said: "I cannot stand the sight of that idiotic boy any longer. He is a pest and a headache." Ahn-Gook was indeed a disgrace and a shame to the honoured family of Kim Sook. Then one day the father learned that his cousin Chung was soon to assume office as district judge of Ahndong, a prestigious provincial post located in the Kyongbuk Province of south-eastern Korea. During a visit to Chung, Kim Sook entrusted Ahn-Gook to his cousin, secretly asking him to keep him in Ahndong for good.

Chung took Ahn-Gook with him to Ahndong, and in his free moments he tried to teach his nephew, only to find that Ahn-Gook was indeed a hopeless case.

"What is the matter with you, Ahn-Gook?" asked Chung. "Strange as it may sound to you, uncle, I can memorize every little bit of a story if I hear it just once. When I listen to stories, I feel that my mind becomes as clear as can be. However, uncle, when I sit down and face letters, not

---

● David Kwang-sun Suh is professor of theology at Ewha Women's University, Seoul, Korea, and a member of the PTE Commission.

only do I get a headache but also I cannot understand a thing. In fact, I get a headache as soon as someone asks me to study. I am prepared to die if you want me to, but please, uncle, do not force me to study." Upon such a pitiful plea from Ahn-Gook, Chung had to give up the hope of teaching his nephew.

One day Chung heard about a well-bred daughter in the household of Yi Yoo-Shin, the township administrator. He sent word to Yi Yoo-Shin proposing marriage between the two youngsters. Administrator Yi thought it odd when he was first contacted. A son of a well-known noble family of Seoul wanting to marry the daughter of a little-known local civil servant! Simply unthinkable. So he quietly inquired if the young man was born out of wedlock. Chung confirmed the fact that Ahn-Gook was a legitimate son of his cousin Sook. Could he be crippled or physically defective, Yi asked. The answer again was "no". Chung called Ahn-Gook in and presented him to Yi Yoo-Shin: he was nearly seven feet tall, very handsome, and had a beautiful voice. What a handsome city boy! Could he by any chance be impotent? He wondered but did not dare to ask. Yet Chung, quickly reading his mind, ordered Ahn-Gook to pull his pants down: the member was in order. Now Yoo-Shin's puzzlement and hesitation grew all the more.

Chung decided to give up the whole deal as he saw there was little chance of convincing Yoo-Shin. However, he thought he would at least clear Yoo-Shin's puzzlement. Chung confessed that his nephew had a learning disability and that his angry cousin had cast Ahn-Gook out of his sight for good. The situation being such, Yoo-Shin thought quietly: "Fancy my daughter getting married to the first son of such a well-known government official. What luck! How can I expect him to be learned?" He then agreed to the marriage proposal for his daughter.

Three months had passed after the wedding. Ahn-Gook would only stay in his bride's room, refusing to go anywhere. So the bride, a little embarrassed, asked him gently one day: "My husband, why is it that you would neither study nor go out of this room?" Ahn-Gook frowned and answered: "Up until the age of fourteen, I could not learn the abc. You know that I was a disgrace to my family and that is why I am living here. Now is it going to be your turn to get at me? I cannot learn any letters. Besides, I get a splitting headache the moment somebody asks me to study. Would you please spare me this pain." The bride sighed. She had no choice but to obey the groom. Days passed by without any change whatsoever in his behaviour. The bride, deeply worried, once again cautiously brought up the subject. "Would you not like to go out to study?

There with my father and brothers you may study and have fun compos-ing verses." But the suggestion made Ahn-Gook angry. "Do you not remember that I forbade you to mention anything about studying? Oh, my head!" He then went to bed with a severe headache.

She was disappointed but she did not say another word. It so happened that the bride was an exceptionally intelligent person and well-versed in both classical and other forms of art. Yet she could not teach her husband as it was against the common practice for a woman to teach her husband to read. After long hesitation and much pondering, she said to herself: "Since he is afraid of studying, I will tell him a story and test his intelligence." So she said to him: "Would you like to hear a story or two?" The groom's eyes sparkled with joy. The bride thus told him a story, into which history was carefully interwoven, starting with the founding of the nation. Ahn-Gook was all ears. She told him part of the story and then asked him questions to find out whether he understood the story. He could recite it word by word without any mistakes or omissions. She, over-joyed, said to herself: "Despite his intelligence there must be something that prevents him from learning." She kept on telling him stories includ-ing numerous classical ones.

One day the groom asked: "Where on earth did you learn all these interesting stories?" "Oh, they are all written in the books. All I had to do was to read them," she said. "Is that really so? Do you think I too can read these stories if I learn how to read?" No sooner had he expressed his interest than the bride brought the books and opened them in front of him. She started to read while her fingers pointed out word by word, line by line, the stories he already knew by heart. That was how he started to learn the letters, the abc. At one try he learned what he had not been able to master up till then. In a few years' time he was an excellent scholar. He took the government service examinations as suggested by his wife and passed with distinction. His father was surprised at the news. His uncle Chung, having heard the secret of it all, said: "It is his wife who succeeded where we failed. We men could not achieve what a woman could."

Stories: the language of Minjung

This story of Ahn-Gook is an old Korean story. It was recently retold by the late Suh Nam Dong (1918-84), the founding father of Minjung theology, just before he passed away in July 1984.[1] It is one of the

---

[1] Suh Nam Dong, *In Search of Minjung Theology* (in Korean), Seoul, Hankilsa, 1984, 301ff. (my translation).

satirical stories included in *Dongsangking chan*, a classic Korean story book published in the second half of the eighteenth century. This particular story of Ahn-Gook was meant to criticize the learning of the time, pointing out how the artistocratic families of the kingdom had been obsessed about gaining and maintaining wealth and power through learning, and how Korean children were forced to study by the greedy parents who only thought about their family prestige and social recognition. People love to hear this story again wherever education is distorted and corrupt, and where "deschooling" is badly needed.

The Minjung theologians in Korea have a more theological interest in the story, because the act of telling the story itself and the contents of this particular story give an important clue to understanding the style of doing theology by the people. First of all, the language of theology. In this story of Ahn-Gook, the boy was forced to learn Chinese characters, which was the lot of all learned Koreans. People, especially scholars, had to learn Chinese characters, Chinese grammar, Chinese prose and poetry, to be able to pass the civil service examinations and to secure a government post. Korean scholars were totally dependent on Chinese, linguistically and, therefore, ideologically.

By the time this story was told in the Old Kingdom, Koreans had already developed an excellent Korean alphabet, grammar, and prose style. They had produced poems and novels which were entirely different from the Chinese. But the uniquely Korean letters were despised by the scholars. To them, the Korean language was vulgar, fit only for oral communication. It was only for women and children, the unlearned. The story is told orally and written in Korean (vulgar letters) by the people, the Minjung, the unlearned, the oppressed, despised and alienated. This particular story of Ahn-Gook was about a young woman, a Minjung, a Korean housewife, who was supposed to know nothing, to have learned nothing, and whose name was not even worthy of mention.

This story of Ahn-Gook does not tell us what kind of stories his young wife told him, day in and day out. She might have included fairy tales and folk stories, some anecdotes and perhaps the stories of the nation — how it came to be and how it had developed, and who were the heroes of the nation and who the enemies. I am sure she told him not only amazing stories, but the painful stories of the suffering people. She might have made him laugh and cry, feel angry and feel sad. The stories she told him were of the experiences of the people, the oppressors and the oppressed, the winners and losers, men and women, masters and slaves. She must have told him of the experiences of winning and losing, of suffering and healing, pain and joy, life and death. Stories are the embodiment of people's experiences. And their stories are the socio-political biography of the people.[2] According to the Ahn-Gook story, the young woman was able to educate her husband and to help him read the Chinese characters. But I am sure that in the process, she made him sensitive to the people's stories. She conscientized him with the stories of the people.

Stories of Minjung theology

The Minjung theology of Korea has taken its name as theologians and young workers, students, priests and pastors met together and told each other stories over food and drink. Friends gathered together secretly in eating places, not to discuss some great theologian's recent writings on systematic theology, but to exchange rumours. Prof. Ahn was taken in by the Korean Central Intelligence Agency for interrogation. Many young female workers who demanded their legal leave were beaten up by hoodlums hired by the company. The university students staged a large-scale demonstration only to meet brutal tear gas bombing by the combat police and the indiscriminate arrest of students and professors. Some tough guys high up had a shoot-out at the end of a big argument, and there soon will be another coup, etc., etc.

Minjung theology has been formed to tell the stories of the Minjung, the people, the suffering teenage female factory workers, the students who were court-martialed, the university professors and newspaper reporters kidnapped and abused in the torture chambers of the Korean CIA. Minjung theology has been formed in the stories told and the rumours spread among the fighting and suffering people of Korea in the 1970s. These stories were forbidden to be printed in the newspapers. Anybody who talked in public about student demonstrations and professors' arrests and young workers' strikes would be sent to jail on the charge of spreading "false rumours". The true stories of the people were censored, while false stories of development and national security dominated the front pages of the Korean news media. The Korean Catholic poet Kim Chi Ha, who was once sentenced to death because of the poems he wrote, said that poetry writing is a sort of spreading of false rumours.[3]

---

[2] Kim Yong Bock, "Messiah and Minjung: Discerning Messianic Politics Over Against Political Messianism", *Minjung Theology*, ed. CTC, CCA, New York, Orbis, 1983, p.184.

[3] Kim Chi Ha's comment was reported in Japanese papers soon after he was released from prison in early 1975. His poetic play, *Gold-Crowned Jesus*, and other writings have been translated into English and are well-known.

As the Minjung theologians listened to the rumours and the stories of the jailbirds, the young workers, the teenage street girls, and the broken farmers — those who were marginalized and outcast in the process of industrialization, modernization and development — they told their own stories in theological statements, declarations of human rights in Korea, and manifestos of Christian faith. As we heard the stories of Minjung told by the Minjung themselves, we thought and reflected on them and spoke from the side of the Minjung, that is, we told the stories of the Minjung theologically and spread the rumours of the people as facts and truth. And we tried to see the world from the perspective of the oppressed and the poor. Through the telling and hearing of the stories and rumours of the Minjung, we were shocked and conscientized and changed; we began to see and feel the world from the perspective of the people. The stories of Minjung have opened the way to the epistemology of the Minjung, the doing of theology from below, i.e. from the side of the Minjung, the oppressed and suffering, the underdogs.

Minjung theologians had to articulate the groans of the Minjung in Korea. As they told the stories of Minjung, they learned not only how to look at the society and the world from the perspective of the Minjung, but also how to tell these stories from a sociological point of view. As Minjung theologians told these stories in socio-political-economic language, they found themselves in the midst of socio-political *praxis*. Minjung theologians' theological language became a body language; the total commitment to their theology became words in action. We saw our actions become events, and we reflected upon these events. We have tried to articulate our reflections in theological language.

In our articulation we have drawn upon contemporary ecumenical theological resources: the political theology of Moltmann, the black theology of James Cone, the liberation theology of Gutierrez, the feminist theology of Ruether, to name only a few. That is to say, these theologians' stories of suffering and liberation became meaningful to us when and only when we spoke our stories — our stories of suffering and of hope for liberation. In our telling of the stories of suffering and hope, we were able to join our friends in the third world to tell our stories of the hope for peace and justice, and ultimately of the kingdom of God. We felt that liberation theology was not like the traditional type of theology that is domineering and irrelevant and therefore only gives us a headache, as in the case of Ahn-Gook. Liberation theology sounded to us like the stories which were told by Ahn-Gook's young wife, and the stories told by our people in Korea. As the stories of our people liberated us from our theology, liberation theology forced us to liberate ourselves from the dependent structure of the dogmatics of the church. From the other side of the church pulpit and theological lecture podium, Korean Minjung theologians related the history of the underside and the stories of the oppressed and the poor.

We have gone deep into the roots of the stories of Minjung. The stories of Minjung we encounter today are rooted deeply in the history of the Minjung of Korea, in their fight against the foreign aggressors, against the landlords, and in their common struggle against the oppressors. Minjung theologians, together with the secular historians, read the history of Korea not as a record of the rise and fall of the dynasties and monarchies from the royal perspective, but as stories of the suffering and struggling Minjung from the point of view of the oppressed and exploited.[4]

In the suffering and struggling history of the Minjung, we found the strong and dynamic culture of Minjung. Korean Minjung have their own "plastic" arts which are not at all plastic, but entirely different from the abstract and mystifying "oriental" arts of the aristocrats. The Minjung performing arts are rough, full of action, erotic, funny, tragic, as in the Korean masked dances. They are performed not as a tourist attraction or for royal entertainment, but outside of the village for the enjoyment and koinonia of the farmers and the village community. The Minjung music is almost always accompanied by story-telling and dancing. The stories of the Korean people were told over and over again in masked dance performances and in the story-telling with songs and dances that are uniquely the people's. The stories of Minjung are performances with voice and body; the telling and hearing of the stories involve the total spiritual participation of the people.[5]

As the Western-trained Minjung theologians began to sing Korean tunes with their (by Western standards) off-key melodies, and tried to dance with their sluggish bodies, they found their cultural roots. They

---

[4] A recently published book, *A Study on Korean Minjung* (in Korean), ed. Ahn Byong-mu, Seoul, Korean Theological Research Institute, 1984, carries a number of articles on "A philosophy of history from a Minjung perspective". It also contains other writings on the history of Minjung struggles, from farmers' rebellions in the eighteenth and and early nineteenth centuries to the Tonghak Revolution of 1895, and to the March First Independence Movement of 1919.

[5] Two excellent studies published in English are Hyung Young-hak, "A Theological Look at the Mask Dance in Korea", *Minjung Theology, op. cit.*, pp.47-72; and *Performing Arts of Korea*, a Unesco Korea publication, 1975.

found their self-identity as *Korean* theologians. This was the experience of liberation: a spiritual salvation as well as a physical liberation. The black American theologian James Cone has observed: "Their affirmation of their own history and culture means that they believe in themselves. The poor can think! They can do theology."[6] That is to say that the poor can do their own theology with their stories, history and culture, and with their own religions. Minjung theology has deep roots in the cultural and religious histories of the people. That is, Minjung theology is not only a political theology but also a theology of the culture of the people. On this, Hyung Young-hak testifies: "God is known and revealing his will in and through the Minjung of Korea, especially the Minjung's history and culture. God was not carried piggy-back to Korea by the first missionary. The Minjung as the cultural proletariat has a messianic significance and role in Korea's history. Beginning to do theology in such a way is exciting; for you feel theology with your body and dance with it before you think it."[7]

Minjung and the stories of Jesus

What is even more important and crucial than the discovery of political theology and cultural theology is our discovery of Jesus among the Minjung. Jesus was with the Minjung and among the *ochlos*.[8] Among the Minjung there were sick people who wanted to be cured and those who were already cured. The crippled, the blind, the deaf-mute — these people were not regarded as normal human beings. They were despised by their families and by the neighbours, and they had no place to go to: they were psychologically, physically and sociologically alienated. The sick people were the social outcasts. The lepers and the possessed were among the crowd of Minjung who could not have jobs, or homes or families.

Among the Minjung who followed Jesus were women. They were mostly nameless, unidentified. But they were close friends of Jesus, perhaps even closer than the disciples. The Jewish tradition would not allow the Christian writers to identify openly who these women disciples were. For even Jesus' disciples did not seem to approve of Jesus having a friendly conversation with the Samaritan woman at the well. What a place

---

[6] *Minjung Theology: People as the Subjects of History*, *op. cit.*, p.xvi.
[7] *Ibid.*, p.54.
[8] The Minjung as the *ochlos* of Jesus is first shown by Ahn Byong-mu, in "Jesus and the Minjung in the Gospel of Mark", *ibid.*, pp.138ff.

for the master to be! (In Korea the well-side is an off-limits zone for men.) And this particular woman had no husband, although she had had five husbands. No wonder the disciples were "astonished to find him talking with a woman" (John 4:27). Jesus not only did away with the old and stuffy tradition and custom, but he seemed to have broken the law that male teachers were not supposed to have female disciples. In the Jewish tradition women did not count. Women were not worthy of becoming the disciples of Jesus. They could not be counted among the twelve tribes of Israel. However, women were at the heart of the Minjung of Jesus.

Jesus was the friend of tax collectors. Tax collectors were collaborators with the Roman colonial government. They were the blood-suckers of the Minjung. They were despised as Roman spies and betrayers of the nation. They themselves knew that they were "filthy rich".

Jesus was with the prostitutes. The prostitutes were despised by their own people not just because they were prostitutes, but because they were tourist prostitutes — they lived on the Roman occupation soldiers and on the so-called pilgrims to Jerusalem from all over the ancient world. The respectable people of Jerusalem would have nothing to do with them, although they exploited the prostitutes and some of them lived on the business.

Jesus was the friend of the sinners. By whose standard were they sinners? Perhaps by the standard of the Roman occupation army. They must have been political criminals — like guerrilla fighters, zealots, and street demonstrators. If these sinners were sinners according to the standard of the Jewish law, then they were the unclean ones, those who did not wash their hands before meals. Perhaps they were the ones who had to break the Sabbath law because they had to work. Perhaps these were the ones who were brainwashed to feel guilty because they did not have enough money to give tithes to the temple. The sinners were the farmers and labourers who had no money and no time to do enough for the temple and the priests. Then they were not "sinners". They believed, nevertheless, that they were sinners, because the rulers and the holy ones defined them as "sinners". But Jesus was their friend.

The good news of liberation proclaimed by Jesus was to tell these sinners that they were not sinners. When he said "Your sin is forgiven", Jesus was saying: "Throw away your guilty feelings because you have only been brainwashed as sinners by the rulers and the religious leaders. Cast that burden away, you are not sinners from the beginning. You are the children of God." These are the liberating words of Jesus. Jesus acted on the side of the Minjung, the *ochlos*, the sinners. Jesus acted like the sinners: he broke the Jewish laws and he had to die on the cross as a Roman political criminal. He was like the Minjung; he stood up as Minjung against the law and against the political and spiritual leaders, proving to the Minjung that he and the Minjung were no longer sinners.

Minjung theologians in Korea learned that at least Jesus did not objectify the Minjung as the object of salvation. Jesus was on the side of the Minjung, and identified himself with the Minjung. This identification of Jesus with the Minjung may perhaps be looked at metaphorically. Sallie McFague's *Metaphorical Theology*[9] is helpful in understanding this identification of Jesus with Minjung. McFague spoke of Jesus as "a parable of God", and as a story-teller. She said: "A metaphorical theology... starts with the parables of Jesus and with Jesus as a parable of God."[10] We have already talked about how the Minjung theologians in Korea took seriously the stories of Minjung. But as to Jesus' being a parable of God, McFague seems to talk about the problem of the identification of Jesus with God.

The important clue to understanding the metaphorical identification is that when one says "x is y" metaphorically, the statement also says "x is not y" just because of the metaphorical character of the language. That is, in a metaphorical utterance, there is this character: "x is y, and x is not y". In McFague's language: "...It is no surprise that Jesus taught in parables or that many see him as a parable of God. For he introduced a new, strange way of being in the world, a way that could be grasped only through the indirection of stories of familiar life which both 'were and were not' the kingdom. And he himself was in the world in a new, strange way which was in many respects an ordinary life but one which also, as with the parables, called the mores and conventions of ordinary life into radical question."[11]

Could we say then that our identification of Jesus with the Minjung is a metaphorical one? That is, Jesus was Minjung, and at the same time Jesus was not Minjung. And Jesus is the parable of Minjung, and Minjung is the parable of Jesus. Only in this light can we understand the story in Matthew 25. The Son of Man in his glory said: "When I was hungry you gave me

---

[9] *Metaphorical Theology: Models of God in Religious Language*, Philadelphia, Fortress Press, 1982.
[10] *Ibid.*, p.18.
[11] *Ibid.*

nothing to eat, when thirsty nothing to drink... when I was ill and in prison you did not come to my help..." (vs 42-43). No wonder the goats protested: "Lord, when was it that we saw you hungry or thirsty... or ill or in prison, and did nothing for you?" (vs 44). These goats' basic problem was they they did not know the metaphorical identification of the Son of Man with the Minjung; for he said to the goats: "I tell you this: anything you did not do for one of these, however humble, you did not do for me" (vs 45).

The Minjung theologians in Korea found the stories of Jesus in the stories of our Minjung. The stories of Jesus were the stories of the Minjung. The history of Jesus, his death on the cross, and his resurrection, is none other than the history of the Minjung. Therefore when we are asked to "define" Minjung or to give the "conceptual" definition or "class" definition of Minjung, we may just tell the stories of Jesus and sometimes give a social biography of the Minjung.

When a rich young man demanded that Jesus give a definition of "neighbour", what Jesus did was to tell him the story of the Good Samaritan. When the disciples of Jesus repeatedly asked Jesus to give a conceptual definition or perhaps an ideological definition of the kingdom of God, Jesus always told them stories. Minjung theology is a story theology in the sense that it takes seriously the stories of Jesus and Jesus as the story of the Minjung.

Minjung should be found in those people who are economically exploited in the factories run by the multinationals. Minjung are those who are sentenced to prison because they were hungry and because they raised their voices against the police and against those who have money and power. Minjung are those who have been deprived of their civil rights, of regular jobs, and of their basic human rights — for political reasons. Minjung may be those who are regarded as lower than human beings just because they had the wrong parents and because they belong to the wrong sex. As a class, perhaps they may be proletariat, but Minjung would include those who do not even know that they are proletariat. As a nation, the neo-colonized people of the third world may be called Minjung. Minjung can be an individual, a family, a class of people, a group of people, a race and a nation as a whole.

Doing theology by the people

But the Minjung carry a common story, that is, the story of Jesus, who lived for others, who suffered and died on the cross, who fought against the forces of death and won the victory of the resurrection. In this sense the "Minjung" is not only a sociological category carrying with it a socio-political biography, but it is also a theological one. Metaphorically the stories of Minjung and the stories of Jesus are common and identical.

Both the stories told by the Minjung about their own experiences and the stories told by Jesus are shocking to Minjung and non-Minjung hearers alike. McFague observes that the stories of Jesus have the characteristics of indirection, extravagance and secularity.[12] The stories of Minjung and of Jesus are shocking because they assault the dominating ideology. In McFague's words, they are assaults on "the social, economic, and mythic structures people built for their own comfort and security".[13] The content of the stories told by the Korean Minjung and the parables of Jesus would turn almost everything upside down. They have an entirely different understanding of reality. Therefore, the Minjung carry an epistemological privilege which the rich and the powerful do not possess. Our theology may perhaps be saved by such a theology by the people who have the epistemological privilege of seeing reality correctly.

In the parables of Jesus, the Minjung inherit an eschatological privilege as well. The prodigal son gets better treatment than his nice and righteous brother. The beggar Lazarus sits in the lap of Abraham while the rich man suffers in the eternal fire. Only the poor and street bums were invited to the great supper. In the kingdom parable, the rich do not become richer and the poor poorer. The parables of Jesus tell us of an entirely different vision of social order where the Minjung are the centre. Blessed are the Minjung, they shall inherit the kingdom of God.

With these privileges and powers of the Minjung, epistemological and eschatological privileges of the people, theology will only be possible when done by the people. In other words, on these Minjung's epistemological and eschatological bases, and only on these bases, can a theology be possible. To use Preman Niles's words, only in the confluence of two stories, i.e. the stories of the people and the stories of Jesus, will the people's theology come alive.[14] The stories told by the people in their suffering and praxis to change the world, that is, the socio-biography of the people, and the stories told by Jesus about the kingdom, that is, the

---

[12] *Ibid.*, p.44.

[13] *Ibid.*, p.45.

[14] Niles's "Introduction" to the Orbis volume of *Minjung Theology, op. cit.*, p.2. Also see "Some Emerging Theological Trends in Asia", *CTC Bulletin*, CCA, Vol. 2, Nos 1-2, March 1981, p.10. Niles speaks more in cultural terms. "...we have come to recognize the fact that we inherit two 'stories'. One is that of the Bible which comes to us through the church and more specifically the Western missionary enterprise. The other is that of our own people and culture" (*CTC Bulletin*, 9.10).

theological biography of Jesus — these are the bases and foundations of theology by the people. The theology of story-telling or the theology of rumour-mongering is the privileged way of doing theology by the people.

I would like to close this reflection with a quotation from Suh Nam Dong, who first proposed this theology of story-telling as a method and characteristic of doing theology by the people.

> If the conventional theology is transcendental and deductive, the story theology is an inductive theology, or a counter-theology (*Gegen Theologie*). Moreover, the conventional theology is a rulers' theology (*Herrschende Theologie*). Having joined and later merged with the ideology of domination, it justifies the ruling order and carries out a function of blessing such orders. They are the letters, books, and systematic theologies. God's transcendence, omnipotence, omnipresence, the sovereign power of Jesus Christ and all that stresses power are the product of political imagination (rulers' language) of the ruling structure. Rulers' theology defended power by making it ever stronger and permanent...
>
> Originally God's revelation took place among the people of Canaan and Galilee... It is their stories. It is by no means theology, but their life stories, and for that matter, it is a counter-theology. It is a counter-theology because the Minjung's stories were aimed at criticizing and correcting the ideologies of domination, the ruling system and culture.[15]

---

[15] *Op.cit.*, pp.305-306, translation mine.

VII

A Chinese Perspective

Kwok Pui Lan

Kuen Kuen has no mother. Her mother died. She was then thirty-five. She used to be strong and healthy, but she died, died of high fever. Yes, she died, with eight others, the day they arrived in Hong Kong.

Kuen Kuen was only three, too small to understand what happened to her Mom. She only knew Mom was thirsty and there was not enough fresh water on board.

They had been in that small boat for four weeks before they arrived in Hong Kong. Kuen Kuen's father spent seven taels of gold for each member of the family before they could leave Vietnam. Leave for fortune, for good? Who knows? But Mom died the very day they landed.

Kuen Kuen, her father and brother lived in the closed camp in Hong Kong. Pa used to joke and tell stories after work. But he did not go to work now, and he did not laugh.

Days, months, years, they waited to leave the camp, to be accepted in one of the Western countries. Here they are now, in the Chinatown of Boston. Kuen Kuen goes to school, comes back home, eats her supper alone, because Mom is not there any more and Pa has to work long hours in the Chinese restaurant.

A sad story? Yes, very sad. Just another story from Vietnam? No, I heard the story myself; Kuen Kuen's father goes to the small Chinese congregation at Boston with my family. It is not just their story, but is intimately tied up with my destiny, as a citizen from Hong Kong, and now with the Chinese community in Chinatown, and in the wider context of the American people.

What sense can we make of such stories? But as James Cone said, we cannot make sense of people's suffering, because there is no answer that

---

● Kwok Pui Lan teaches religion and society at Chung Chai Theology Division, the Chinese University of Hong Kong.

faith can give for suffering that removes its contradiction. They do *not* require a theodicy from us; faith cannot explain evil. It empowers us to fight against evil.

Theology by the people begins with the stories told by these people. We heard the story, cried with them, felt the hurts and tasted the wounds. Only then could we struggle with them to put the broken pieces of life together, to try to figure out the voice of God speaking through the tears and sighs, murmurs and laments, anguish and hope, no matter how dimly it comes through.

People in diaspora

C.S. Song once said, the history of the people of Israel serves as the sign for all other peoples. The great event of the Exodus, the triumphant entry into Canaan, the separation of the kingdoms and the final exile of the people to the foreign land serve as a transparent prism through which the judgment and the salvation of God can shine through.

What is the particular element in that history which speaks to the present suffering of the Chinese people? I would say it is the scattering of Jews in diaspora. I am not at all sympathetic with what the nation of Israel has been doing recently, but the longing, the dream, the hope to be one people can be shared by all Chinese, especially those Chinese who live away from the motherland.

There is a saying in Chinese: "The tree grows to 10,000 feet, the leaves fall and go back to the root." The Chinese in Hong Kong want to go back to the root, and so do the people in Taiwan, the Chinese in Southeast Asia, the Chinese in Vietnam in particular. What hinders them from going back?

The story of the tiny pearl of the Orient, Hong Kong, suddenly occupies news headlines. Mrs Thatcher signed the agreement with Premier Zhao on 19 December 1984 concerning the future of Hong Kong. *The Boston Globe* said: "British Prime Minister Margaret Thatcher signed *away* Hong Kong yesterday." Why *away*? To the people of Hong Kong, Hong Kong never belonged to them. As the majority of the people, in fact 98 per cent, are Chinese, the people of Hong Kong should be glad to return to China. Why did the counsellors go to Britain to pursuade the members of parliament that they have "moral responsibility" over Hong Kong? They cannot come as they like and leave as they wish. Why did group after group go to Beijing to channel the so-called opinion of the people? Why are the people afraid to go back to the motherland?

To be a people, for those who have been separated for so long, is never easy. There are ideological differences, a great gap in living standards, and vast differences in socio-political structures. Hong Kong people used to say, we don't have democracy, but we have freedom. And we are not certain we can have such freedom, not to mention democracy, in the days to come. To affirm we are one people calls for the courage to say we are one in spite of the differences, the commitment to put your own destiny on trial with the larger whole, and the vision that guides us through the storms and upheavals.

The post-exilic prophets pointed to a day that Yahweh will gather the sons and daughters of Israel, and the nations will be judged and will know Yahweh is God. Whenever a people is brought together, whether Chinese, Koreans, Germans, Vietnamese, there will be both the judgment of God over the forces that separate them, and the grace of the Lord that finally brings them together as a people.

Women as part of the people

The suffering of the boat people is the suffering of the women. Kuen Kuen's mother was a refugee from China. She followed her father to go to Vietnam after the Second World War in search of a better future. At the age of 16, as a young girl, her marriage was arranged by her parents. At 17, she gave birth to the first child, who died shortly afterwards because of poor sanitary conditions in the village. She then gave birth to two other children, and hoped they could live and grow in Vietnam.

The political situation of Vietnam changed so rapidly. It was beyond her understanding. Many wealthy Chinese people started to leave. Kuen Kuen's father was only a small businessman and they hoped to stay on. But the situation became more and more critical, and when Kuen Kuen's father sold everything to buy gold so as to get a place for the family in the boat, his wife had no choice but to follow him.

They were lucky that they did not meet the pirate ships as many small boats did. Kuen Kuen's mother had heard about the stories of rape and robbery, and she was very afraid. She had also heard that people threw little crying children into the sea lest their boat could be located by the police or the pirates. The results are the same: women raped, men brutally hurt, property seized.

Kuen Kuen's mother felt sick on the seventh day. She was prepared to fight the pirates but not against shortage of water. She had high fever, and she couldn't even cry. People cry when they are in misery. For her, it was more than misery. She was confused and could not make sense of it, neither could the seventy people on board who saw that some of their relatives were dying just because of the shortage of the most basic thing: water. The taels of gold in their pockets could not save them, all their valuables were useless. O God, if there was a God; what an irony!

Before the final moment came, she panted and gasped. Summoning all her strength, she held Kuen Kuen's hand, gazed at her and said: "Kuen... Kuen, lead a better life... Don't live a life like mine..."

When she died, her eyes would not close. People say if one dies unjustly or if one has some unfinished tasks in life, one cannot close the eyes and go. For her, it must have been both.

"Don't lead a life like mine!" What a parting statement! But it is more than that. Her last words are a powerful accusation, yes accusation, from the people's point of view. Many women in Asia must have uttered such words to their daughters, though not in the same miserable situation. These words which represent their most treasured and deepest hope spring from that very womb that once nurtured their children. Child, have a better life, live a life healthy and in peace...

Women are more than half the population in Asia, but they do not hold up half of the sky. They are withheld from participation in the political and public realms, and hence their fate and destiny are to be decided by others, not shaped by themselves. Kuen Kuen's mother submitted to her father when they ran away from China, and she listened with wide eyes when her husband said they must leave Vietnam again. She might have to depend on her elder son if the pirates came and Pa Pa got hurt.

Theology by the people? By whom actually? We do not hear the voices of these women, these poorest women who are mostly illiterate and cannot even tell their own stories. Are these women not counted among the people? Yes, probably, women were also present at the feeding of the five thousand, yet they were not counted (Matt. 14:3-21)!

"Lead a better life..." Those words do not speak to Kuen Kuen alone, but to all Asian women, toiling and suffering. Stand up straight, be a person. Doesn't the Chinese character of "human being" mean standing up? Did Jesus not relieve you from the infirmity that caused you to be bent over for eighteen years (Luke 13:10-17)? Stand up, tell your story, shape your destiny, we cannot tell what the merciful God has done, without your help.

People in solidarity

Kuen Kuen's mother died, but Kuen Kuen has to live. Can she ever forget the horrible night when they left Vietnam, can she ever recover from the pain of seeing her mother dying? Will she grow up as a "healthy" girl? What kind of fortune awaits her in Boston?

Kuen Kuen will be growing up in the Chinese community, among the newly emigrated people who came from China, Hong Kong and other parts of Southeast Asia. Ethnically speaking, they are all Chinese. But people can easily detect the difference by the way one speaks and dresses. Everyone knows the Vietnamese-Chinese have the saddest story, but who wants to hear the bitter history and to rehearse the bitter memories that many emigrants share? Who wants to be associated with the poorer sector of the community and not to look up to the more wealthy?

Kuen Kuen's very presence in the United States is a very powerful testimony. She is a living witness of what one nation has done to other poorer nations. American people have very mixed feelings towards the Vietnamese. Their conscience tells them they are morally responsible for the suffering of innocent children like Kuen Kuen. But their sympathy, on the other hand, also goes to those American young men who lost their lives in Indochina.

These good-willed Americans also cannot understand why they were caught up in the war with Vietnam. They knew so little about this small country, and the American universities can hardly find qualified persons to teach Vietnamese. Yet the country was involved in the war that made thousands homeless, killed so many and stirred up such violent student movements and resentment.

Kuen Kuen, now nine, cannot understand all these ambiguities. She only knows Mom died and Pa Pa and brother have to go to work early and come back late at night. She goes to school, comes back home, eats her supper alone.

Will a poor little child like her have a better life? Can the younger generation expect a brighter future from us? The picture is gloomy. Young people in Asia cannot foretell their future because of political and economic instability, American youngsters cannot say they have a future at all because of the crazy competition in nuclear armaments and the so-called weapons of "life".

Our hope cannot be left to be worked out by those who have power. Our destiny will be at stake if we submit ourselves to the mercy of others. People in every part of the world must come together, we have to fix the broken pieces of life and try to create a better human community that can make sense. There is no time for pondering and bewilderment. Do you not hear the words of the arrested Filipina activist and poet, Mila D. Aguilar:

Have I touched your life,
Has the wind from the mountain of my soul
Rustled through your leaves
Like mayas on a ledge
Moving like rhythmical mannequins
Have I rested your eyes?
After the first torrent
Amidst a sky foreboding futher ill,
Has my chirping chipped the stillness.
Tell me, have I given?

VIII

An African Case Study

Rosario and Agustin Batlle

Presented in this paper is a method that emerged in a situation of doing theology by the people. It is a method that enables the empowerment of the people to express what God has done in their life and what we can learn from it.

Cultural manifestations of the African Independent Churches

The African tribal groups in general have this structure: everyone has his/her own place, his/her own model, his/her own duties and obligations in relation to the rest of the group. There is also the consciousness that every member of the tribal group has the duty to keep "the harmony" of the group and this harmony is maintained in the relation that everyone has with the spirits (the good and the bad spirits). Whenever a member of the group breaks that relation, that person must pay for all that he/she did wrong, in order to appease the spirits that are causing harm to the community. It could also be a tribal offence, not just an individual offence.

Everyone in a tribe is responsible directly to the spirits. This is the reason why there is no priestly caste *per se* in the traditional tribal system. A person can become possessed by the spirit and it is shown by certain signs. Being possessed is a sign that he/she (usually he) has had a special call. That person becomes a candidate to receive special initiation in subjects such as healing, divination, etc., and to serve the community spiritually and materially. The person is also given the symbolic instrument of the office, then becomes a priest(ess). There is, therefore, no

● Agustin Batlle, a Chilean in origin, is currently Director of Theological Education by Extension Training for the African Independent Churches. This programme is an arm of the Organization of African Independent Churches based in Nairobi, Kenya. Batlle is a Presbyterian pastor. His wife, Rosario Batlle, works with him. Originally a Chilean, she is now a US citizen. She is a graduate of St Paul's Theological College, Limuru, Kenya.

special caste, for the spirit can come to anyone irrespective of class or sex. Although the priest(ess) is trained to know the secrets of appeasing the evil and good spirits through sacrifices, etc. there are religious functions which most members of the community can and must perform. Almost everyone can pour libation upon sacred rocks and graves, calling upon the ancestors for protection before a journey, the setting up of a business, planting, childbirth, etc. In some cases they can perform sacrifices even if they are not priests.

Thus the priest is what we today call the "enabler", the one who assists because he/she knows the secrets of the trade and leads the community in the important task of maintaining harmony between its members and the members of the world of spirits. It must not be forgotten that the world of spirits is the intermediary between the people and the one God who is the creator and sustainer of all creation.

The Independent Churches mirror something of this in the roles people play in the church; everyone is responsible for being faithful to God in his/her duties and responsibilities. The church structure in most of these churches operates the same way in that there is no priestly class, although some Independent Churches do have a hereditary caste that in many instances is now raising the problem of the succession of leadership. Some church heads inherited the leadership from parents or grandparents. "Some people say that the next head of our church must be the son or grandson of the Prophet (the founder)." This is the case, for instance, in Kenya (African Israel Church Nineveh), Ghana (Musama Disco Christo Church), Northern Transvaal, S.A. (Zion Christian Church), Zululand, S.A. (the Church of the Nazarites), Lesotho (the Berean Bible Readers Church). Other people in these churches say "we need elections", and divisions follow.

The theology of the African Independent Churches

As Mbiti has pointed out, their theology is an oral theology expressed in singing, dancing, preaching, healing, prophesying, casting out of evil spirits, prayer and conversations. People feel free to rejoice openly and freely in the power of the Spirit — the same Spirit that is there and here and all over the world. There is spontaneity and participation in liturgy in their theological expression. And among these indigenous churches, Christian faith is not limited to Sunday worship; their faith is a way of life, as it was also for their pre-Christian ancestors. These churches have discovered support in the Bible for traditional African ways of under-standing the world and relating to God. By returning to the traditional forms and practices, they provide their followers with a familiar African context for the biblical claim that God has sent his Son Jesus Christ. (This does not mean that we are unaware of distortions, ideologies, hidden biases, and the admixture of cultural elements which are foreign to Christian teachings.) The verbal expressions are in accordance with African tradition which values oral expression. The participants in doing theology in these churches are the lay people, the women, the young, the old, children, and the clergy. All are recognized as capable of making their contribution.

Orientation of ministerial formation

It is in the expression of theology in the African Independent Churches that one sees that theology can be done in community rather than by a few bishops or teachers or prophets. Each individual of the group shares in the hymns, prayers, etc. There is no competition, there are no specialists. But today these church groups are realizing that experience is not enough, and many of them are turning to theological training, with the setting up of the Organization of African Independent Churches (OAIC) in Cairo in 1978. There is a concern for leadership training through the method known as TEE. In the late 1980s the OAIC/TEE programme was organized and has been operating from an office in Nairobi with an advisory committee. The heads of various Independent Churches or their representatives have been serving on the OAIC/TEE advisory committee.

The task of doing theology by the whole people of God is expressed also in the OAIC/TEE programme. It gives an opportunity to all: young people, women who have always been marginalized, and men who are not leaders, lay preachers and pastors, bishops, etc. From the bottom to the top everyone may have the training opportunities to study the Bible. This is a corporate enterprise which involves all the people of God and not just a few that represent the group. This corporate learning enterprise is also in accordance with African tradition that puts emphasis on corporate life. This theological community is also the one that decides on the theologial priorities which need to be studied (or discussed).

OAIC/TEE relevancy, meaningfulness and viability

It is a pioneer training programme. It has dealt with people who have had no opportunities for study, much less for theological education. It has also started from zero level, at the point of "discovering the Bible". This TEE programme has begun at that level because it has wanted to be relevant to the needs of the people. Being *relevant* also means that if people had nothing before, they should begin from almost zero. And that was why we started with a basic text called "Discovering the Bible". Being *meaningful* means that these people have not been turned off by what these early texts have given them. Not everything is new to them but to these known things have been added unknown things. They have found that they understand; that they are learning new things that will help them to be better church leaders, things to teach their people. This method is *viable* because it is a method which depends on the participants themselves to help each other to learn and because it has also taught them that they can teach each other, that they do not need an enabler with a doctor's degree, only someone who keeps ahead of the participants, who can share with them new information and knows enough biblical theology to keep them on the right path.

Besides this role of resource person the enabler has the additional task of acting as dialogue motivator on a specific study subject or theme; the person must also help them to relate learning to their own lives. This does not require a graduate from a foreign school of theology. The TEE programme is viable because the people who are served can be enablers in their own parishes, and they are also students. We are using their facilities as study centres. They themselves provide room and board for the participants and for the TEE enabler, therefore there is no expenditure which they or the OAIC/TEE programme cannot handle. The TEE office in Nairobi covers travelling expenses of the TEE worker (in Kenya). In other African countries with whom we are in relation, different arrangements are found depending on each situation. But the principle is the same everywhere: we try to involve the participants as much as we can in the practice and cost of their own education.

We think that one new insight that has been gained is that a training programme like the OAIC/TEE does something new for certain church groups. This TEE programme has contributed to a theological education that is *relevant* because it does not leave the participants behind, but helps them just where they are so they find in the programme what they are looking for; it is *meaningful* to them because they do not feel that they have been introduced to things they cannot handle, it is *viable* because it does not call for expensive staff or new physical facilities.

Participants are full participants in their own education. They pay for their travel expenses to the study centres, and room and board. The training is a joint adventure. They have not been given anything free, they are contributing to their own education.

The OAIC/TEE model of doing theology

With Agbeti we define doing theology as the interpretation of a people's experience of God, and God's dealing with them in their history. Such theology is systematized in Judeo-Christian tradition and unsystematized in the oral tradition of black Africa.

In the TEE study centres in Kenya it is understood that when participants are reflecting on a subject or issue, they are doing theology because they are saying how God is working in their life (or situation) as pastors, as leaders, or as church members. And this happens constantly in our TEE study centres. It can also be a model of congregational renewal where not only does the leader speak but also the group that gathers together to reflect on what they have experienced in their life. I am sure that this happens in many other places, but no one has told them that they are doing theology. They themselves do not believe that they can do theology; they think that only specially trained people who are officially appointed can do it for the church.

In the groups that gather as TEE study groups, we realize that within the dynamic of each group, things are happening when each person in a group starts seeing him- or herself as someone who has an important story to share. In many of these groups people begin by waiting for the "teacher" to stand up and dictate the content of the course. Then they begin to realize that the seminar leader has changed his/her role, that now he/she is an enabler and not a lecturer, and they are called upon to give their opinions. Then they go through those moments of doubt about what they should say: "Are the other members of the group interested in listening to me? If I say something, how will the leader react? Will he/she react the same way my former teacher did when I was a child?" Every member of the group sees him/herself in a different way, he/she is no more one of the "mass" but someone who also has a story to share, and whose story is important because the group considers that everyone in the group is important. And it is there that congregational renewal begins.

The OAIC/TEE programme — an adventure

The OAIC/TEE programme is an adventure, it is something that has not been done before with the groups we are dealing with. We have discovered that we have not been able to imitate what was done elsewhere because of the different needs. We realize that what is happening here in Africa has necessitated a different approach to work with different people and situations. So what has been achieved by the OAIC/TEE so far in theological education is a new development. Each day, since we arrived in August 1980, has brought situations that we have never known before. First of all, our task was to enable them to want to see us (or making attractive the idea of meeting us), and eventually meeting them. From that first meeting evolved a training programme that has had to deal with particular needs and situations which we had not accumulated in our experiential baggage.

What will be the future of this venture? It is very difficult to say how far we can go because the possibilities are enormous. There is no way to know where they will lead, because we have not begun to cover or to deal with the 7,000 or more Independent Churches in the African continent. Out of all these churches, we have only been dealing with 50 in Kenya (a country with more than 250). It has taken us four years to do this, which does not include the TEE consultation work in many other African countries. We have been able only to give introductory training in Bible and other subjects and about the principles and methods of TEE, on how to use them and what that can do for them. We have been trying to find human resources in the other countries that can continue the work we have initiated there: some person or some institution that is willing to collaborate in training the people who have approached us in Nairobi. Our task is to discover who and where these church groups are that want training; to know what they want and what resources are around them that can meet those needs.

Our three-month training programme of TEE workers from outside Kenya is also contributing to equipping more TEE workers who will make a contribution to the TEE cause among the African Independent Churches in their countries.

A possible model of doing theology by the people for congregational renewal

We believe that one of the ways to incorporate this new way of doing theology for congregational renewal is through the creation of TEE study centres within the church (in a diocese, or district, or presbytery, or congregation). It is within these groups that the congregation — Protestant and Catholic — is going to be renewed while they do theology (or reflect upon what God has done in their lives). It depends on the groups themselves to record this, and help their congregations to catch the vision of doing theology by the people.

Congregational renewal is possible when every person is an "important person" and every group values its members. The process is this: "They ask me a question, I don't know if I will answer it because if I give a wrong answer I'll be scolded. But the enabler notices it and tells me that there is nothing wrong in answering the way I want, that what I am going to say is my own authentic experience and that all of us want to learn from it. It seems to me then that I am not going to be scolded, when for the first time I give my point of view, my reflection, and I realize that the people respect me, then I feel motivated to learn also from others, and to reflect on what other people say and accept it or not, the same way others did with me." And it is here, where a person's growing process begins as part of the group and brings renewal to the group, that repercussions become possible throughout the church.

IX

Theological Education Among
the People: A Personal Pilgrimage

F. Ross Kinsler

One of the critical needs of our time and of every era is to encourage, enable, equip and empower the people of God to participate meaningfully and fully in the life and mission of the church. One of the tragic ironies is that the very institutions, structures and resources which were created to facilitate people's participation have so often failed to do so or have even become obstacles. At times it seems as if established patterns of ministry, church order, and theological education conspire with social, cultural and economic factors to produce and perpetuate dependence. The ministry of the church is coopted by professionals; witness and service lose vitality; worship is performed by a few and observed or abandoned by most; and faith becomes irrelevant or non-existent.

The Spirit of God has never been bound by our institutions and structures, of course. Reform and renewal movements have transformed, bypassed, or rearranged the church's furniture so that great numbers of God's people could participate genuinely in its life and mission. Nevertheless, we are called to mould and adapt our institutions and structures to be channels and not obstacles for God's Spirit.

Over the past 21 years I have been intrigued, challenged and surprised by the possibilities for reform and renewal through theological education by extension. This model of theological education opens up all kinds of questions and establishes many new relationships, which in turn can lead to unexpected changes, opportunities and understandings. It is no panacea; it can cause complex problems; there have been failures. But in many places it is a useful key to unlock the leadership puzzle and release the dynamics of participation in the church.

● Ross Kinsler, formerly an assistant director of the Programme on Theological Education of the WCC, is currently on the staff of the Southern California Extension Centre of the San Francisco Theological Seminary.

My own education about theological education began with 13 years in Guatemala, where I was challenged constantly by opportunities and needs, issues and problems, colleagues and context. We learned on the run. Then I joined the World Council of Churches' Programme on Theological Education, and for six years my ecumenical horizons were stretched, particularly with regard to the actual and potential role of theological education. During the last 18 months I have had the opportunity to test these learnings in Southern California.

I would like to share this personal pilgrimage as a case study. I do not intend here to put forward an overall philosophy or scheme for the reform of theological education but rather to reflect on concrete experiences. I shall focus on extension as a model of theological education that encourages, enables, equips and empowers people to participate in ministry, mission and theology. I see the extension model as one way of dealing systemically and not just peripherally with the problem of participation, which is a problem of the whole church. I believe theological education by extension is a vehicle and a movement for change whose potential we have barely begun to realize.

Ministry by the people — the Guatemala experience

The story of the Presbyterian Seminary of Guatemala's extension programme has been recounted many times. At this time I would like to focus on the nature and significance of the changes that took place when theological education was made accessible to virtually all the people in that particular context.

First, many people enrolled. The former residential programme averaged 10 to 20 students, mostly young, unmarried and inexperienced. The extension enrolment soon grew to 150, then 250, and even 350, and these students were a cross-section of the whole church. Perhaps most significant was the way that the natural leaders, who were mostly mature, married, experienced in all realms of life, came to the fore, whereas previously they had been largely excluded. This meant not only that the church could equip and empower its most capable leaders but also that the leadership would represent the people as never before.

Second, our church was able to continue and greatly expand its outreach. According to our Presbyterian polity, only seminary-graduated, ordained pastors may administer the sacraments; in Guatemala very few local congregations could pay a full pastor's salary; most of our congregations had never had a full-time pastor. On the other hand, we discovered that elders and deacons and young people and "ordinary" members were witnessing and serving so effectively, even where the itinerant pastors visited only occasionally, that the congregations were multiplying by leaps and bounds. By taking theological education to these people, the seminary strengthened the spontaneous expansion of the church. Many more congregations were established; ordained and unordained leaders were trained for them; new presbyteries were organized.

Third, the church grew in diversity and unity. The old seminary in Guatemala City had for 25 years provided a middle-class, middle-level, schooling experience for ministerial candidates; Bible institutes were established to serve our two major Indian constituencies; the cultural, educational and socio-economic scope of entering students and graduates was very narrow. By contrast the extension programme was only limited by the imagination of its leaders and the durability of their vehicles. Centres were organized in the hot coastal planes and cool highlands, among highly educated professional leaders in the capital and equally competent though less schooled or unschooled leaders in the Indian and Ladino towns and villages. Different academic "levels" and approaches were necessary, but we insisted on the functional parity of our courses and certificates. All the students were enrolled in the same institution; they gathered at the rural headquarters for periodic study conferences; and they marched proudly side by side at the annual graduation celebration.

Fourth, the clergy-laity dichotomy began to break down. In our system local church boards interview and recommend candidates for ordained ministry, who are then "taken under care" of presbytery until they complete their preparation and are called to serve a church. Under the new arrangement only about 25 per cent of our students entered theological studies with the intention of seeking ordination; both candidates and non-candidates carried out many pastoral responsibilities during the entire period of their studies; as they progressed, some non-candidates were encouraged to become candidates and vice versa. A few presbytery leaders continued to insist on a sharp distinction between the two groups — with the implication that candidates for ordination were somehow more important and the rightful business of the seminary. Our concern was to equip the people for ministry and to overcome this dichotomy.

Fifth, theological studies became relevant as never before — not primarily through the skill of the teachers but through the realities of the students. Theological education by extension is preparation in the context of ministry, not just preparation for future ministry. As adult education specialists all over the world have noted, adults bring to learning a wealth of experience and understanding and motivation which can never really be created or simulated by schools. Insensitive teachers and irrelevant texts and inappropriate curricula can, of course, block or distort this new potential for integration of theory and practice, theology and life, but extension teachers and students are constantly challenged to make these connections directly and immediately.

Sixth, a natural consequence of the previous factors was that the meetings of students and teachers became more dynamic than anything we had ever experienced in our own schooling. Because extension classes were held at each centre just once a week for two or three hours, we eliminated lectures and developed materials and methods that enabled students to acquire the basic course content on their own. They came to class prepared to discuss their lessons and their experiences with each other and with the professor. Dialogue was spontaneous, genuine and serious. The teacher provided additional academic expertise and stimulus; the students provided expertise and relevance and diverse points of view out of their congregations and communities.

Seventh, the process of learning and equipping did not stop with those who were enrolled in the programme. It was inevitable that they should utilize what they were learning in their local situations, not just when assigned to do so but simply because it was the best use of their time. Courses in inductive Bible study provided abundant material for preaching and teaching, and the reports of their experiences added excitement and meaning to the classes. In some courses we designed the study materials in such a way that the students could use them to teach a group of elders, Sunday school teachers, etc. In other courses we asked them to prepare lesson plans, sermon outlines, etc. This further demonstrated that we were partners, educating the church for ministry.

Eighth, we eventually realized that we were developing channels that could enable the whole church to gain new understanding, deal with critical issues, and face new challenges. In the past some church leaders had challenged the seminary for requiring courses in psychology; then we offered the pastoral psychology course to a group of pastors in that region and their perspectives changed dramatically. Protestants generally had a closed mind towards the Jehovah's Witnesses, Mormons, Seventh Day Adventists, and especially towards Roman Catholics; our course required students not only to read books about these groups but to talk with them, visit their worship services, and make their own evaluations. Only men are ordained as pastors and elders in the Presbyterian Church of

Guatemala, but many of the extension students are women, so the ground is being laid for their full participation in leadership.

Ninth, perhaps the most important factor was the change and development of relationships which are the key to learning and participation and spiritual life. We have mentioned that theological education by extension in Guatemala opened up new relationships between young candidates and mature leaders, leadership training and the growth of the church, preparation and the diversity of leaders, clergy and laity, teachers and students, learning and experience, learning and teaching others, theological education and the current agenda of the church. Symptomatic of all of these is the new relationship between the seminary and the church. When student representation on governing bodies became an issue in the US in the late sixties, we looked at the membership of our seminary's board of directors and discovered, not surprisingly, that half of them were students, simply because our students are leaders at all levels of the church's life. It was not unusual to have moderators and clerks of presbytery or synod in our classes.

Finally, these changes represent a movement towards "ministry by the people". One observer suggested that the Presbyterian Seminary of Guatemala committed "institutional suicide" in order to break out of the academic-professional-elitist captivity of traditional theological education. At one time I proposed the name "open theological education" in order to put the emphasis on access and participation. Our vision was to open up the full range of theological education and ministry to women and men, young and old, candidates and lay persons from all parts of the country, all educational and socio-economic strata and all ethnic groups. This vision began to become a reality as all kinds of people enrolled in the seminary's extension programme. But it continues to face resistance because it runs against so many assumptions about education, leadership, theological education and theology.

Conclusions

The theological foundation for the Guatemala extension programme was the affirmation that ministry is the vocation of the whole people of God. We found ample biblical and historical grounds and ample pragmatic evidence for that affirmation. It follows that our patterns of ministry, church order, and theological education must be critiqued and reformed in order to encourage, enable, equip and empower the people of God to participate meaningfully and fully in ministry.

Our assumption was that theological education can open the door to full participation for all sectors of the church by providing a decentralized programme adapted to the realities of people in their diverse situations. This led us into a process that continues to reshape not only our programme but also our understanding of theological education. Opening theological education to the people creates new possibilities for ministry and also for mission and theology.

Others who wish to explore similar possibilities in their own contexts are encouraged not simply to adopt an extension model but rather to ask themselves basic questions such as the ones we have raised here.

— What is your theology of ministry, particularly with regard to people's participation, and how does that theology challenge existing patterns of theological education and elitist tendencies of your church and cultural context?

— Are your churches and their leaders fully representative of the people who live in your local and regional context, especially women, racial-ethnic minorities, the unschooled and less schooled, and the poor?

— Have you examined the current and possible alternative relationships between theological education, ordained ministry, leadership, and the people in your denomination?

— Does your pattern of ministry and theological education challenge and equip people not only for service to the church but also for outreach into all fields of human need?

— How does/can theological education integrate life experience, academic preparation, and leadership in ministry most effectively?

Mission by the people — the Geneva experience

While on the staff of the World Council of Churches' Programme on Theological Education (1977-83), I was able to observe developments in theological education by extension in all regions of the world and also to explore its relevance for various sectors of the church's mission. Following is an enumeration of some of these sectors which offer vast opportunities for the people of God to participate.

1. As I had observed in Guatemala, the church has been expanding rapidly in many third world countries, and this expansion is unrelated to formal theological education. It was during this time that we began to hear that the majority of Christians are no longer Europeans and North Americans but rather Africans, Asians, Latin Americans and islanders of the Pacific and the Caribbean. In third world regions the work of ministry is mostly carried out by the people and their natural leaders, not by trained professionals. In the other regions the number of active members is

falling, even where there is an abundance of ordained pastors and priests. In parts of all regions it seems as if growth is inversely proportional to the level of theological education of the leadership. Theological education by extension is being adopted in third world countries as an appropriate way to equip the large numbers of natural leaders with much-needed theological tools rather than to ignore or bypass them, and in some first and second world countries it is being introduced to provide advanced pastoral studies for clergy, theological formation for laity, and basic ministerial training for marginalized people.

2. Our attention has increasingly been directed towards the poor. We now realize as never before that God's concern for the poor will have to become a priority for the church, that the poor not only receive the good news but become bearers of the good news, that the church must not only preach to the poor but also be evangelized by the poor. This is particularly important for theological education which, by utilizing dominant schooling models and levels and standards, is moving as rapidly as possible away from the poor, even in the poorest countries. The extension model offers, as we have noted, the possibility of making high quality theological education available to all, including the poor, without extracting or alienating them from their own people and also without imposing on them a hierarchical understanding of education and credentials.

3. For many years the WCC's office of Urban Rural Mission (URM) has been in touch with groups of Christian workers all over the world who are engaged in struggles for human rights, social and economic improvements, and human dignity. Their guiding principle, which has been confirmed again and again by experience, is that the people themselves must organize, identify their needs, and participate in the decisions that affect their lives. Many theologians have begun to reflect on the relationship between God's rule and human struggles, but few theological schools have explored the possibility of utilizing this model of education through action. Since theological education by extension does not remove the students from their life situations, it could incorporate the basic URM approach, and human struggles could become basic material for theological and ministerial formation.

4. Another department of the WCC works on development issues and relates to groups engaged in self-development in different parts of the world. While governments and corporations increase their control over economic and social institutions, the overwhelming evidence is that material, technical, and human resources are not being used for the good of the people, that few benefits trickle down to the majority poor, whose

numbers are increasing rapidly and whose plight is becoming even more urgent. Research in global food and hunger reveals that every nation could produce sufficient food for its own people, and community development programmes demonstrate that the people are capable of meeting their own needs. Once again we must ask how the church can equip people for this vital dimension of human need, and once again it appears as if theological education by extension is ideally suited for this task.

5. New developments in the field of health care are closely parallel to emerging concepts of ministry by the people and offer a particularly cogent challenge to theological education. Having examined the inadequacy and injustice of health care systems that depend heavily on professionals and institutions and exclude large sectors of the population, the WCC's Christian Medical Commission and the World Health Organization have given first priority to community-based, primary health care systems. Local committees identify needs and supervize their own programmes; local health promoters are trained by extension, apprenticeship, or intensive short courses; emphasis is placed on preventive medicine, health education, and community development. Theological education by extension has the capability of training local health promoters and also of creating a new theological understanding of the church as a healing community, with enormous potential for health care service in industrialized as well as developing countries.

6. In most countries education is imparted through a closely regimented hierarchy of grades and certificates that lead to corresponding levels of economic benefits and social privileges. Schooling is promoted as the principal cornerstone for democracy, but more careful analysis reveals that schooling often serves to rationalize and reinforce injustice and exploitation. Paulo Freire's approach to education as liberation meets people at the bottom of the socio-economic pyramid and challenges them to discover their autonomy, their rights, and their humanity where they are. Theological education by extension can incarnate this philosophy of education in terms of the church's ministry, and it might also help the church to discover a new vocation, more radical than its traditional institutional approach, in the field of education, for the purpose of building a more just society.

7. In the field of science one finds another parallel in the development of appropriate technology. Edward Schumacher's *Small is Beautiful* exposed many of the myths of the corporate and bureaucratic approaches which have been centralizing power, abusing the environment, and dehumanizing people at an alarming rate in recent years. We now know

that alternatives are available, that local people can design and manage agricultural and industrial operations that are more productive, more ecologically sound, and certainly more human, to the benefit of all. The question arises as to the role of the church in this important dimension of life and more specifically the role of theological education. Extension networks could include such issues in their curricula and thus challenge church leaders in relevant occupations to exercise new leadership as an expression of their Christian vocation.

8. World attention has been drawn to the extraordinary growth and witness of the Christian base communities in Latin America, Africa, parts of Europe, and elsewhere. Some churches and many movements have begun as people's movements, but sooner or later they create structures and institutions that result in elitism and dependence. We must ask whether theological education by extension can help to spread and sustain the dynamic participation of the people by keeping open the doors to leadership. The base community movement could then continue to recreate the churches from the bottom up.

9. Theology itself is being recreated around the world as Christians of Africa, Asia, Latin America and elsewhere give verbal and non-verbal expression to their faith in the context of their historical and cultural contexts. Equally significant are the emerging feminist expressions of our common faith. These new contributions have been called liberation theologies because they express the centrality of human liberation and also because they liberate theology itself from the biases and narrowness of inherited formulations of the faith. The incarnation of the gospel in faithful living and contextual theology is the responsibility of the people of God in every time and place. The challenge to theological education, particularly theological education by extension, is to give the people the vision and the tools for this endeavour.

10. Finally, all these observations — and many others that could be added — seem to call for the reordering or re-creation of the ecumenial movement from the bottom up. A critical issue for every aspect of the ecumenial agenda, every sector of human need, every frontier of the church's mission is people's participation. Even such milestones as the Faith and Order convergence statement on "Baptism, Eucharist and Ministry" and the new ecumenical affirmation on "Mission and Evangelism" will be merely symbolic unless and until they are taken up by the community of faith at the local level. Theological education, like other structures and agencies of the church, has usually operated from the top down, but theological education by extension offers the possibility of joining hands

with recent developments in other sectors to form a popular base for the ecumenical movement under the banner of "mission by the people".

Conclusions

This persistent probing of the people's role as the primary agent of mission finds theological roots in such biblical concepts as the body, *shalom*, and *koinonia*. The Hebrew-Christian perspective on human nature emphasizes wholeness and corporateness, which are essential for justice and peace. Koinonia means not only community but also sharing and participation. From this perspective all social pyramids and hierarchies must be converted to the service of people's participation.

Our assumption is that theological education, which has generally followed the elitist, hierarchical tendencies of the dominant cultural systems, can in fact be counter-cultural and utilize alternative models in order to pursue its primary goal, i.e. to encourage and equip the people of God for ministry and mission. The case for an extension approach to ministerial formation is strengthened remarkably by the parallels we now see in fields as diverse as evangelism, development, health care, appropriate technology, and liberation theology. Pragmatic concerns and wholistic understanding of human needs both suggest that theological education by extension should be utilized to present a full-orbed vision of the church's mission and to equip the people for their ecumenical vocation in all areas of life.

Church leaders and theological educators who wish to explore this challenge may want to grapple with questions such as these:

— What does your theology of mission say about people's participation and about the church's responsibility towards the whole range of human needs?

— Do existing patterns of theological education equip clergy and laity only for ministry in the church, or do they also challenge a wide diversity of people to utilize their gifts and faith for service and witness in their social and occupational worlds?

— What are the critical needs in your communities, and how might local congregations become channels of healing and justice for those communities?

— Is there any realization among your members that they can and should generate their own theologies out of their experience of the gospel in relation to their struggles for full humanity?

— What does the ecumenical movement look like from the perspective of the members of your churches... and what might it look like?

Theology by the people — the Southern California experience

By the time I came to Southern California, I had edited a collection of reports of 29 extension programmes in different parts of the world under the title *Ministry by the People*, and I had drafted a paper on "Theology by the People" with the intention of pressing colleagues in different places to examine the theological significance and substance of their attempts to do theological education among the people. I had also begun to reflect on the manifold facets of the ecumenial agenda as a Rubic cube of opportunities to engage God's people in mission. I was invited to become the director of the Southern California Extension Center of San Francisco Theological Seminary and soon discovered that the entire ecumenical agenda was latent in that extraordinary context and that I was being asked to explore the full range of possibilities for theological education there. The following reflections come out of my first 18 months in this new situation.

1. San Francisco Theological Seminary has been developing new patterns of theological education during the last 25 years. In 1961 it introduced a long-term, field-based degree programme for practising pastors, called the Doctor of the Science of Theology, which was the precursor of the shorter Doctor of Ministry, which some 80 US seminaries now offer. In 1974 the seminary introduced the Master of Arts in Values, a degree programme designed to equip lay persons for Christian vocation in their diverse professional and social settings. And in 1979 SFTS, which is the only Presbyterian Seminary west of the Rocky Mountains, began to establish extension centres for the theological renewal of the church among the western states. The seminary now has approximately 200 resident students on campus, most of them taking Master of Divinity studies in preparation for professional ministry, and about 800 off-campus students in the STD, D.Min., and MAV degree programmes, plus a large number of persons who participate in a variety of continuing education programmes through the five extension centres. The shape of this institution has changed enormously during this period; the impact that these changes will have on the ministry, mission and theological renewal of the church is not yet clear.

2. The Doctor of Ministry programme is administered by the San Francisco office 800 miles to the north, but our Southern California Extension Center helps to recruit new candidates and organize them into local collegium groups. Each group (7-11 persons) goes through thirty weeks of weekly seminars, a six-week summer intensive on campus, additional two-day seminars close to home, and the dissertation/project

(D/P). The latter requires extensive research on some aspect of ministry and often leads to significant experimentation and learnings that benefit not only the candidates themselves but also their congregations and the wider church. One D/P which I evaluated recently was an analysis of the experience of a large and influential, but shrinking urban congregation and a new conceptualization of the local church as a confederation of diverse peoples, interests and programmes in a pluralistic context — an alternative to the homogeneous principle of church growth advocates and a challenge to the biases of class, race and culture in our denomination. The candidate will present his findings to his congregation and also to a regional consultation on "What does it mean to be faithful? Theologies and models of church growth."

3. The Master of Arts in Values programme is entirely decentralized. Local collegium groups (10 to 15 persons) take — on a part-time basis — a series of 11 courses on various aspects of the study of values with a Judeo-Christian foundation, then go through a values analysis exercise, take four additional courses, and embark on a thesis/project (T/P) on some aspect of their vocational/advocational involvement. As potential values change agents, most participants work on the meaning of their vocation in the world outside the church. One of my students is, however, the unordained minister of music in a large Baptist church, and her T/P hypothesis is "that if the laity are involved in the planning and the implementing of the worship service, the experience will be more significant and relevant to them as they struggle with value issues in their everyday lives". She has tested this hypothesis by forming a lay worship team and holding weekly seminars with them to develop their theological understanding and incorporate their perspectives in the planning, execution and evaluation of Sunday worship over a ten-week period. Now in its second cycle with a second group of lay persons, the model will be presented to the district churches and to a wider audience through a denominational journal.

4. During the past year we completed the first series of intensive seminars for the Certification of Associate Christian Educators. Designed to provide biblical, theological and educational foundations for professional and non-professional church educators who have had no opportunity to take formal studies in this field, this programme prepares them for the denominational qualifying examinations for certification. My particular concern has been to strengthen the recognition of these persons as partners in the theological and ministerial formation of the church. This first group of candidates includes several presbytery-level consultants

who have great ability and experience already, so when we came to the seminar on the educational programme of the church, they taught each other the course by preparing and presenting case studies on specific areas of educational ministry from their own work. After further refinement of this model with Christian educators I would like to adapt it for church musicians, youth workers, and perhaps church administrators. These are all areas of primary importance for the most basic theological formation of the church.

5. The most intriguing aspect of our work in Southern California is its multicultural and international context. Although this is an Anglo-dominated society, there is now no majority population in Los Angeles county or city. We estimate that there are about four million Hispanics, one million blacks, one million Asians, and hundreds of thousands of Samoans, Israelis, Arabs, Iranians, Armenians, and Native Americans. Due to the immigration and evangelistic outreach of non-Anglo Presbyterians, the number of predominantly non-Anglo congregations in our synod has increased from 2.5 per cent to 30 per cent during the last 12 years. Current reports indicate there are now more Presbyterians in Korea than there are in the US, and there are probably more Korean Presbyterian congregations than Anglo-Presbyterian congregations in Southern California —though most of the Korean congregations have not joined our ecclesiastical structures.

Perhaps the greatest opportunity for the theological renewal of our church lies with these racial-ethnic constituencies because they experience the gospel and view the world from different perspectives. The Black, Hispanic, Japanese, Korean and Taiwanese leaders have already organized theological academies that offer lay courses, lay-clergy seminars, and conferences to equip their people within their cultural heritage for service in a pluralistic context. Our centre cooperates in these endeavours and co-sponsors seminars to awaken the wider leadership of our church to the spiritual and theological riches now available in our midst. Some Anglo leaders have already been awakened by witnessing for the first time the power of Black preaching, taking a series of seminars on the Hispanic reality in this country, or by hearing a Japanese-American compare the Asian concept of *wa* with the Hebrew concept of *shalom*. We can now begin to challenge the Anglo hegemony of our church in order to create a truly multicultural church with a global perspective.

6. The main task of the Southern California Extension Center is to provide continuing education opportunities for clergy and lay persons. This functional definition includes a variety of activities — seminars,

conferences, lectures, retreats, workshops — that do not carry academic credit. One of the specific foci for our continuing education events during the last 18 months has been "Christians and the Crisis in Central America", the theme of a major report of our denomination that was released just prior to our arrival in Southern California. The synod of Southern California and Hawaii endorsed the report in the fall of 1983 and commended it to all our churches for study, prayer and action. The following spring our centre and synod co-sponsored a regional conference on Central America with the participation of a resource team from Central America. Then in July we co-sponsored a travel seminar to Mexico, Nicaragua and Guatemala. The 11 participants, who had been deeply moved by the witness of Christians and by the intervention of our government in Central America, gave approximately 100 presentations in our churches and presbyteries during the next six months. In September 1984 we organized synod's task force on Central America, and together we invited Richard Shaull, a former professor at Princeton Seminary who had just spent six months in Nicaragua and had just finished two books based on his experiences there, to be our theologian-in-residence for studies on the crisis in Central America, during January, February and March 1985.

During this three-month period Dr Shaull taught an intensive course on "The Gospel and the Poor: Christian Responses in Central America and the USA" at three locations in Southern California. He made presentations at seven presbytery events, two presbyterials, three meetings with pastors, five clusters of churches for Bible study, and ten local churches. In addition he led a synod retreat, gave keynote addresses at nine ecumenical events, made 17 appearances at 11 universities, and visited three seminaries.

There is no doubt that these activities have increased, broadened, and deepened interest in Central America. In fact the timing could not have been better both in terms of current international and domestic affairs (e.g. threats against Nicaragua and indictments of sanctuary workers) and in terms of recent resolutions by our church concerning Central America and sanctuary for refugees. Many of our people have learned a great deal not only about the situation but also about the biblical understanding of poverty, oppression and liberation, the experience of Christians in the struggles of Central America, the role of the US government, and the responsibility of US Christians — with implications that reach far beyond Central America.

The commitment and involvement of some has increased to the point of considering basic changes in life-style, seeking a new kind of community for nurture and support, and taking stands against the dominant cultural values and power structures of our society. If God's preferential option for the poor is the critical gospel paradigm for our time, then those who choose to join the new reformation may have to make many changes in order to side with the poor, live with the poor, or even become poor. Our exposure to Central American base communities and refugees indicates that people who choose this calling face opposition, suffering, and even death, but they also experience liberation, profound hope, and genuine community.

7. One specific kind of continuing education that we have not yet developed fully is one- to two-week programmes for clergy study leave. Pastors in our denomination and others are normally expected to spend two weeks per year in some kind of education for their ongoing ministry, and they may go to a seminary, conference grounds, etc., for that purpose. In July our Center will co-sponsor with synod and Occidental College a nationally advertised event called "Worship '85". Intended for pastors, choir directors, musicians, worship committees, and others who design and lead worship, the programme will include convocations on preaching and worship, seminars and workshops on prayer, pastoral leadership, organ, handbells, choral techniques, repertoire sessions and choirs.

8. Another major area of concern which we have just begun to explore is the urban context. Southern California has become the major cosmopolis of the West, the most influential urban area in the country. We have initiated conversations with sister institutions and denominations about the educational potential of our context; one proposal is that we create a centre for urban theology that will design and coordinate learning and theologizing experiences for all kinds of people on an ecumenical basis. Pastors and lay leaders, seminarians, D.Min. and MAV candidates should be offered a variety of programmes that will inform and transform their understanding of life and ministry in this extraordinary urban context.

9. Without a clear strategy in mind the Southern California Extension Center has become a partner of the Synod of Southern California and Hawaii, its several programme areas, ten racial-ethnic constituencies, eight presbyteries, and 310 churches. Our concern has been to respond to current needs and issues in the life of our church, i.e. to find ways to educate the church theologically in response to current needs and issues. Some consider the central task of theological education to be professional training for new candidates, and we are exploring the possibility of

designing an alternative M.Div. programme for Southern California. But we are also seeking to establish a new understanding of theological education through which a broad base of the church's clergy and lay leadership can deal more directly with the complex and often controversial problems of church and society — as with the Central America issues.

10. When the operating committee of the Southern California Extension Centre drew up a paper on its vision for theological education in Southern California, we identified five major goal areas: ministry and theology by the people, contextualization of the gospel, unity of the church, justice and peace, and *koinonia*. All five goals converge in the formation of ministering, caring communities that seek healing and wholeness not only for themselves but for the whole world. We are committed to serve the worldwide church of Jesus Christ through the formation of those who in turn will equip and lead the local church with a global vision. It is in relation to these two foci, the global community and the local congregation, that the seminary forms people for ministry, witness, unity, justice and peace.

Conclusions

In my paper "Theology by the People" I have argued that theology is primarily the work of the church, the people of God, because it is reflection on the incarnation of the gospel through Christian discipleship in every time and cultural setting, in human life and struggles. This may sound simplistic; it should certainly be self-evident. The tasks of theology are to explore and articulate the faith, to distinguish faithfulness from non-faith and disobedience, and to teach the faith to each new generation. These tasks must necessarily be undertaken by the community of faith.

My very limited experience in Southern California indicates that there are innumerable opportunities to encourage and equip people for the fundamental and urgent theological tasks that rich and powerful North American Christians must undertake. Some pastors are engaging in the theological education of their congregations, but it appears as if few are willing or able to challenge the cultural, ideological, class, and racial captivity of our church. Most of our people, even within our racial-ethnic constituencies, continue to pursue or submit to the values of individualism, wealth and power that are deepening the poverty and alienation in this country, causing untold suffering and death around the world, and accelerating the expenditure of the world's resources on the tragic illusion of security through armaments. The significance of our work must be measured ultimately not in terms of activities and programmes but in terms of human transformation under God's rule.

Those who wish to pursue these concerns may wish to deal with questions such as these.

— What are the critical theological issues your church must deal with at this time?

— How can the whole church at all levels be challenged to face these theological issues as integral to their faith?

— Do existing theological education programmes deal with these issues and equip a wide base of the church's leadership to do so?

— What old and new programmes might contribute effectively to this process?

— Is human transformation taking place in response to these issues under God's sovereign rule?

X

Perspectives from Latin America

Jorge C. Bravo

Today we are conscious of the fact that theological mission cannot ignore the people with all their anguish and their life of poverty and humiliation caused by those who wield the power.

God, while making the covenant with Abraham (Gen. 17:1-8), indicates the wish to establish a special relationship with the chosen nation: "You shall be my people and I shall be your God..."

Jesus Christ, when announcing his ministry (Luke 4:16-21), emphasizes the type of mission that he will realize: a popular ministry, non-traditional, with the poor, the marginalized and the oppressed of this earth. The church has often neglected this popular element in its mission and instead compromised itself with its preference for the privileged sectors of society, forgetting the great existential conflicts of the suffering people.

Thanks to the influence of the Holy Spirit in the life of communities of faith, these have in several ways been including the suffering people in their reflection and ministry and have opted to become involved in different situations, such as: the right to life and human rights; solidarity with the poor and marginalized; the proclamation of justice, love and peace. Also, they have denounced all types of violations that threaten the people. A phenomenon that has motivated this commitment of the Christian communities is the irruption of the poor and marginalized into the life of the community and into society.

This reflection from the communities comes forth in the midst of a suffering, hungering and thirsting people. *Suffering*, because centuries of pain mark our people —from the time of the European conquerors up to

---

● Jorge Bravo is coordinator of Programa Metodista para la Capacitación (PROMESA), a programme of theological education by extension of the Methodist Church, Lima, Peru, for lay leaders and pastors.

the present governments who in turn represent the interests of the great powers. *Hungering*, because the bread does not reach the most humble table; many pass the whole day without tasting a piece of bread, and our men, women and children die each day. There is hunger in every sense of the word because there is also spiritual hunger. Our people need to nourish themselves with the bread of life which is Jesus Christ. *Thirsting*, because the vital element does not reach their pitchers. Dehydration is epidemic in many humble towns. Many children die because of this illness. Also, our people are thirsty for the word of God; they want to drink from the spring of living waters.

In this way, our theological work is influenced by the daily life of our people, who have suddenly begun to make their presence known in the centre of our communities of faith and we, the pastoral agents, want to share with them a theology for life and not for death. It is because of this that we want to sketch guidelines for "A Theology for the People".

Characteristics of a theology for the people

1. It must be biblical. The basis of our faith, and consequently, that of the mission of the church, is found in the holy scriptures. In them we find the source of our faith and of our work. We also find here the will of the Father and the teachings of Jesus Christ. These can be summarized in the verse: "Seek first the kingdom of God and its justice..."

The fundamentals of our reflection and mission must come from reading and re-reading the Bible in the context of the experiences of our people. Our faith must come from our daily experiences with God and with our neighbour. Therefore, opting for the poor and marginalized is a result of a re-reading of the biblical message in response to the irruption of the poor and marginalized in the heart of the church, which in turn is caused by the situation of death and oppression in which our Latin American continent lives.

In this situation the word of God must open the way in the darkness. As the psalm states: "Your Word is a lamp to guide me and a light to my path" (Ps. 119:105). In this sense, the biblical characteristic seriously conceived is fundamentally transforming and has the potential to effect a permanent renovation of the church and its mission. On the other hand, this biblical characteristic does not permit merely an emotional approach to the scriptures, but a rational reflective approximation which is in keeping with the capacity of human thinking. This, then, is what theological reflection is.

Finally, a biblical-theological reflection assumes that one will approach the scriptures with the contributions of all the scientific resources on hand in order to be able to interpret our reality — of oppression and death in this case.

2. It must be dialogical. Educational philosophy has long known that education cannot consist of a handing over of knowledge from the one who teaches to those who learn, but that it is a product of exchange among the different participants in the process of education. It is an exchange that is not limited to the imparting of knowledge but also to the sharing of experiences.

This implies that all theological reflection and mission, being an educational process, should take into account this attitude of dialogue. The church must also keep in mind this attitude of dialogue and should not merely enter into dialogue with other churches; it must be in dialogue with current schools of thought and with the suffering people, following the practice of Jesus. In this sense dialogue and the attitude of dialogue are profoundly evangelical. The biblical message and the message of Jesus do not simply take a single direction. There is not one sender and one receiver; the roles interchange. In practice, Jesus evangelizes in the contexts of the authentic dialogues that happen within concrete situations lived by those who come into contact with him.

The church should promote this attitude of dialogue in all its mission in the world, be it through its reflection or through its work. It cannot be assumed that people, especially those who are poor and marginalized, are "empty", with nothing to share. The gathering of all their experiences and expectations will enrich the ministry of the church and will give it new horizons in its mission.

3. It must be for the service of Christian identity and cultural identity. All reflection and theological mission of the communities of faith should be for the service of those who are less fortunate, the dispossessed and marginalized of society. But this reflection and mission should take into account the issue of Christian identity and the affirmation of the cultural identity of the people. *The Christian identity* needs to be preserved in all the affairs of the communities of faith; it should not be diluted among the different scientific and social doctrines of today. We are Christians because we have been converted to Christ and follow in his footsteps, we are not merely "instruments" or "agents" of change who are influenced by some doctrine, but to us is entrusted the good news of Jesus Christ for all of humanity. Let the world not confuse us with followers of social doctrines or political theories. We are faithful to the gospel when we make our choice — in this case for the poor and marginalized in our society.

To emphasize our Christian identity is not to say that Christianity is exclusive in the area of the liberation of our people; it signifies identification with the word of God in the midst of the process of liberation.

In terms of *cultural identity for the people*, it is necessary to lay emphasis on the uniqueness of each people's culture, that is, each one's cultural expression. One's culture should not be destroyed through the influence of other cultures. All reflection and theological mission should bear this aspect in mind and they should originate from the continuous exchange of experiences within specific cultures. In the case of Latin America, each country has its own cultural traits, but there is a common axis in the pastoral task and that is the religious fervour in the life of each people and their situation of misery and dejection.

4. It must be committed to the poor. All through the Old Testament God is presented as a liberating God, a defender of the poor, the orphan and the widow. God raises prophets from among the chosen people to denounce, announce, and establish justice and peace as the expression of God's love for the poor and marginalized.

God and the people are the principal actors in the Old Testament; they celebrate a pact which implies faithfulness and obedience. That is why God is presented as the one who is eternally faithful to the covenant, and justice, love and peace are the signs of God's saving presence.

The prophets continually point out that one cannot preach the hope of reconciliation in a situation where there is sin and injustice: until there is a radical alteration in the situation, there will be no possibility of lasting change, and this implies punishment and destruction.

Jesus does not neglect this aspect and takes over the work of the prophets and, in a very special way, expresses that it is the will of the Father to establish the kingdom and its justice. He represents in this way the guiding thread of God's conduct: *God's preference for the oppressed and the poor*. He does not limit himself to proclaim liberation for the poor, but he opts for them, for the marginalized of his time (sinners, tax collectors, women, prostitutes, children, those ignorant of the law, etc.) who were not included in the formal theology of that time. But that is not all, Jesus goes further than opting for the poor; he becomes poor, so that his word and practice have weight and authority. Through the centuries the church has not ignored the poor, but it has neglected their total redemption. In the majority of cases it has been on the side of those causing the oppression of the people. And it has utilized popular devotion to guarantee the imperial system.

Today, it is necessary that theological discussion and its ministry become committed in a more radical form to the poor and oppressed of our world, that is, with those suffering and in pain who await their liberation. We must remember that the majority of our people are a believing people who express their faith and devotion in simple forms, even rudimentary forms at times. And yet, in spite of their suffering, they have not lost their faith in the liberating, merciful and saving God.

If reflection and mission are pursued in a context outside the commitment to those who have the least, then they automatically become the elements of an empty, dead theology, instead of a theology that generates abundant life as was the case with the ministry of Jesus Christ.

Perspectives

1. For the service of community fellowship. One cannot live a Christian life of commitment individually, but only in fellowship with the community of faith, which is the body of Christ of which we are members. It is clear that a spiritual life out of the context of the church is an illusion. This is why a "theology for the people" must promote fellowship with the community of faith and with the people. Together people can meditate and share daily experiences in the light of the word of God and of prayer and worship.

The spiritual strength that communities need for the development of their work comes through Christ, when we let ourselves be guided and trust our future to the action of the Holy Spirit.

2. Training for service. The Christian experience is marked by the "feeling of Christ" as is said in the Letter to the Philippians (2:5). It is a feeling of service, according to which the interests of others should be put before our own. The Christian should be a servant to others as was taught to us by our Lord Jesus Christ (Matt. 20:23).

In this same way, all theological training should be oriented towards service, in this case, to serve and accompany our least favoured brothers and sisters; that is, the poor and marginalized who seek their liberation and redemption.

3. Seeking new forms of theological education for the people. A theology for the people implies as well a new method of education for the people. New developments offered by the educational sciences, pedagogy, and especially popular education, and the experiences of the base ecclesial communities should all be taken into account.

This theological education could acquire the following forms: aptitude workshops, workshops for meditation and prayer; weekly meetings for the pastoral agents; experience groups.

XI

A New Stage in the Development of the Christian Community

Elsa Tamez

A new phase

In this short reflection on theology by the people I would like to emphasize the following: from the moment we allow the people to do theology we enter a new profound phase in the development of the Christian life.

Today we are experiencing this new phase in many church communities. It is a response to certain events. First of all, as we all know, the poor, like blacks, native peoples, women and the laity, have decided to stop being invisible in history, and are demanding to be taken into account. Secondly, this irruption of the marginalized has revolutionized many spheres of secular and religious life. For example, in the theological field, the fact of poverty and the poor has been introduced as a subject that challenges and encompasses the whole of theological reflection. The reading of the Bible from the perspective of the oppressed has restored to it its lost meaning. Thirdly, the presence of these marginalized sectors has been a milestone in history, not only because they have become visible and they have made people think about them as an actual reality, but because they also seek to act as protagonists in history. In the case of theology, they demand also to be active subjects in the theological task — they want to do theology.

This last fact, we repeat, marks a new profound phase in the development of the Christian community.

Why is it a new phase?

For many years the people only listened, and received theological knowledge through teachers, pastors, books and pamphlets. The people

---

● Elsa Tamez, originally from Mexico, is now resident in Costa Rica. She is on the staff of the Seminario Bíblico Latinoamericano (SBL); she is a Methodist and a PTE Commissioner.

never thought that they were capable of making theological statements or saying what they thought. Implicitly, it was a task assigned only to specialists. So the people thought about God and about the gospel in the way the experts told them to, but not on the basis of what they believed or their way of viewing reality. As these marginalized people assert their presence, challenge theology and appropriate the Bible to read it from their own perspective, the situation changes. On the one hand, the people are learning to do theology; and, on the other, the theologians, teachers and writers who listen to the voice of God speaking on behalf of the poor, are learning to listen to new things never before heard or read.

Consequences

This theological contribution by the people has had two simultaneous consequences. On the one hand, it has invigorated theological thought in general, and has induced in specialists an attitude of humility towards the academically unqualified. Thus, for the first time in history, a rich dialogue has been initiated in which the contributions of both sides complement each other. On the other hand, the fact that the marginalized sectors are doing theology, i.e. they are thinking about God from their own perspective and in their own way, *has made their faith a living faith*. Their theological reasoning, because it arises out of their own experiences, is more convincing and more meaningful for their Christian life, because theological statements that do not arise out of real life have ended up by becoming facile phrases, empty of meaning. From the moment the people attempt to do theology, a spirituality bursts forth in which there is greater consistence between the daily life and the religious life.

Finally, the fact that the people *say* their theological word and are *heard* signifies a step forward in the recognition of their dignity. When the hungry ask for bread and receive it, their dignity is not necessarily being taken into consideration. But when the people think and enter into theological dialogue, they recover their dignity. In fact to allow people to think, to enter into a theological dialogue (in their own way) and to make their contribution, is also to recognize their human dignity.

In this new phase of the Christian life, which is stimulated, among other things, by the fact that the people are also doing theology, a new vitality is being experienced in theological thought and spiritual renewal among the people; also, new personal values are being acquired such as humility on the part of the professional theologian and dignity on the part of the simple people.

With this new step we are coming closer to the style of life of the Christian communities portrayed in the gospel. How the people do theology, what their contributions and difficulties are, and what is the role of the professional theologian are all subjects to be discussed at length. In the meantime let us welcome this right of the people to do theology.

XII
People at Work

Michael H. Taylor

Theological work

We would not run true to form if we did not get bogged down at some point in definitions, not least in trying to define "theology". I intend to circumnavigate the bog by two routes. First, I suggest it is pointless to define it as if there were some correct definition to which all should then conform. It is not however pointless to be clear what we are talking about and we should therefore begin any conversation about theology by saying not what the word means, but how on this occasion the word is going to be used. My second route round the bog of defining theology is to lead you towards an even worse bog where we try to define the even more slippery term "doing theology". It is bad enough to ask what we mean by "theology", but even more conversation-stopping to ask what we mean by "doing theology". I shall rescue you from this particular bog by telling you that when I speak or think of people "doing theology" or engaging in theological work (the work we are called to re-invent as people's work) I have in mind two closely inter-related tasks for the people: constructing and articulating a faith by which they can live, and learning to live by the faith they construct (build) and articulate. These are the theological dimensions of what we have been taught to call "praxis" or the proper rhythm of Christian living, combining committed action and critical reflection.

People's work

It appears to be a matter of general agreement (though not of course of universal practice) that this work of constructing and articulating a faith

● Michael Taylor, an English Baptist, was until October 1985 the principal of the Northern Baptist College, a college of the University of Manchester, England. He is now director of Christian Aid, Great Britain. He is a vice-moderator of PTE.

by which to live, and learning to live by the faith that has been constructed and articulated, is to be done by the "people", and immediately we are threatened by another area of marshland. If we need not define "theology", we have to decide who are the "people". Are they the poor, the oppressed, the laity, the untutored but naturally intelligent, the academic, the high-ups or low-downs? Are they outside the church and inside other religious communities, or are they confined to Christian believers? Are they of certain ethnic, cultural, social or political groups? What — or rather who — are they? But for the purposes of our discussion there is no need to decide who the people are. The whole point of the phrase "theology by the people" is not to emphasize that no one can do our theology for us. They, or we, must do it for ourselves. It is a protest against people who think more highly of themselves than they ought to think, professional hierarchs and authority figures who have for far too long and far too often thought they could construct and articulate faith for others, and tell them what it is, and teach or instruct them how to live by it. "Theology by the people" has little interest in ruling some in and some out of the human race. It has every interest in a do-it-yourself theology, if not, as we shall see, a do-it-by-yourself theology. We may invariably need to do-it-ourselves in community, but if pushed I should want to insist that I might even have to do-it-myself alone, in that no one can finally tell me what my faith should be. I must have, and live by, my own faith.

Some may be disturbed by my decision not to say who "the people" are (or, better still, perhaps to drop the definite article and simply talk about "people") and by my suggestion that the point of the phrase "theology by the people" lies elsewhere. For some are very concerned to define the people as the poor and oppressed. I have shifted the ground to one dominated by liberal democratic Western values, by laissez-faire and pluralism and freedom of choice, where everyone does their own thing. I am already moving on a totally different map. To insist that people do their own theology may be a liberal value, but it can also be a liberation value which sets people free from the oppression of imposed ways of believing about themselves and their world. The theological work which is people's work could then be most accurately described as the work of "constructing and articulating *our* faith by which *we* can live, and learning to live by the faith *we* have constructed and articulated".

If we ask, "why this insistence on doing it for yourself", a large part of the answer for me is hidden in the word "relativity". It is the relativity of all faiths and all theologies which today we recognize as an inescapable fact, and many have now come to recognize as a cause of celebration since what is relative can also be related and therefore relevant. Any faith that we construct and articulate and learn to live by will take the form and shape it does because it is inevitably related to a number of factors. To take the three most obvious ones, our faith is influenced by the sort of human beings we are temperamentally and psychologically; it is influenced by the culture in which we happen to have our being; and it is influenced by the historical circumstances which press upon us and evoke from us a particular response. If these change, then faith will change; and the fact is that they do change. The growing number of named theologies from "black" to "Minjung" to "Western" are but a tiny part of the evidence that they change, for those interesting groups themselves embrace endless varieties of communities of women and men with their own special characteristics, cultures and circumstances. A faith constructed by other people in other cultures in other times and circumstances cannot be ours.

The only grounds on which we would be right to impose a faith on others, or at least actively encourage them to accept it for their own good, would be if we were in possession of some absolute or universal faith which was not subject to the relativities and relatedness we have just described. Since no such faith exists, not even in the Bible, we are strengthened in the conviction that people must construct and learn to live by their own.

I want to pause here, at this point of agreement, long enough to register two hesitations about this enlightened attitude to people doing their own theology. The first is to note (yet again) that the wolf may have returned in sheep's clothing. Having agreed that "our" faith for example cannot be imposed on others, we may be busy doing exactly what we say we disapprove of by insisting that they construct and articulate a faith of their own. To put it in the standard jargon of our theme, "theology by the people" implies that people need or should have a theology; but perhaps we have to leave it to them to decide. The point is not merely that we should not require of them our kind of theology, whether it is of the rational or narrative sort. The point is that we should be careful not to assume they need a theology of any kind. Suppose, for example, I was asked what "faith" was all about for me. I should reply it has to do with the meaning of human existence including my own life. To suggest that everyone should feel the need to give their life a meaning may be an imposition. Some may regard it as quite unnecessary and pretentious and, if it occurred to them, very modern. The fact is that those who are enthusiastic about theology by the people, and I am among them, may need the people more than the people need their theology.

The second hesitation we should at least register about our enlightened attitude is that it may not always receive the warm welcome we think it deserves. The people may not be pleased by our conclusions. They may not want the gift we take it upon ourselves to offer. They may prefer to have the theological work done for them rather than do it themselves, and many of us doubtless know such communities of people. In other words, the people may need converting as much as we do, a point to which I shall return.

Granted these hesitations, we may register a measure of agreement that the theological work of the people is to construct and articulate a faith by which they can live, and learn to live by the faith they have constructed and articulated. Perhaps we should further refine even that way of putting it and speak about learning to live by the faith they are constructing and articulating, since in the midst of their obedience it is an ongoing task.

Working conditions

Over a number of years I have tried in a very limited and modest way to work with groups of people at trying to discover how this kind of theological work is done. I shall not stop here to report on the method that we have developed, only to note the sort of conditions that need to exist if the work is to be done. If these conditions are met it is not of course inevitable, but it is at least possible and likely that people are about their theological tasks. If they are not met, I do not believe there is much hope that those tasks will even be begun. I shall not seek to justify them, only explain what they are. When I speak of them I tend to have the picture of a local community in the back of my mind, local because it is near to action, not necessarily close to home.

1. First, there must be *commitment to practice*. Theological work has to be done within the setting of active obedience or discipleship. This certainly involves serious commitment to the tasks which God's kingdom requires if people are to be free and truly human; but it involves a rather more ordinary commitment as well, to the everyday tasks which people have to do "in any case" as members of families, workers or non-workers, lovers, players and citizens. This community of theological workers takes seriously and as a matter of the highest interest what people have to do almost without making choices, as well as what they decide they ought to do. Theological work may involve "day-dreaming" but never idle day-dreaming.

2. Second, there must be the *constant confession of faith*. The phrase may be misleading, though not altogether so, for those used to speaking of a confessing church. To confess faith as I understand it here is not to admit you are a Christian, or to recite a creed, but to confess your convictions about your life, what perhaps it means to you, your values and hopes, what matters to you, what comforts and sustains and energizes you. Such confessions may be made in all sorts of ways: visual, verbal and demonstrative, in prayers, poems and stories and careful statements. Theological work cannot be done unless people are prepared to confess what they believe as the raw material of construction.

3. Third, constant *attention* must be paid *to Jesus* as a historical more than a dogmatic figure. Here I am assuming a Christian community, though theological work can of course be done in other communities, in which case attention will be focused elsewhere. The faith to be constructed and lived by is not made up only out of the material to hand. Something comes from outside ourselves. People make something of their lives without Jesus, but Jesus makes something of their lives. There is a gift revealed in the gospel. In any case what makes any faith "Christian" and one with all other Christian faiths is its claim to be a faithful response to One who is the Truth and the Life and the Way. I do not need to point out the complications of paying attention to this Jesus seen in so many different guises and so readily made in our own image. For all that, the community must be evangelical — mindful of the evangel which is Jesus — if its theological task is to be done.

4. Fourth, the community must be not only "evangelical" but "catholic". If it must pay attention to Jesus, it must also pay attention to those other faiths that have been constructed and articulated and lived out of loyalty to Jesus; East and West, historical and contemporary. It must be wide open to *inherit the common wealth of Christianity* made up of the wide variety of faiths which arises because although they owe allegiance to the one Lord they are inevitably and properly related to the changing temperaments and cultures and historical circumstances of which we have already spoken.

I might be expected to mention the presence of the open Bible as a fifth working condition for the theological task. I do of course believe it is a necessary condition but it is an aspect of the last two I have described. Reading it is the principal, though by no means the only way we pay attention to Jesus; and reading it brings us into contact with part of the common wealth of Christianity and some other Christian faiths but by no means all.

I must say that I have been almost shocked by the way in which the Bible has been so prominently featured in some discussions as the most important and productive theological resource we have, if not quite the only one. I have asked myself why it does not feature so prominently in my own thinking. I have wondered if it functions more directly in some cultural settings and whether mine is not one of them. I have wondered whether we have become so aware of the cultural distance between ourselves and the Bible that we have put it virtually beyond reach. (A recent English volume which faced up to this cultural gap was called *The Use and Abuse of the Bible* and left some with the distinct impression that the abuse of the Bible was indeed to use it!) But let me add in favour of my lesser emphasis on the Bible and greater emphasis on the common wealth of Christianity that I am more often reawakened and invigorated in my faith by encountering other faiths (not least the faiths of this continent) than I am by reading the Bible.

5. The fifth working condition is for the community to be as open or *exposed* as it is possible for it to be to *what the world is really like*, which will generally mean how we experience the reality of the world in which we live. At this point the community might be described as a genuinely "lay" community, taking the understandings of the world that are available to us in ways which are not specifically Christian as seriously as those which are. At one level this means paying attention to the sciences, physical and human, social and political. At another level it means paying equal attention to our everyday experiences, feelings, stories, and insights, and those of the other human beings with whom we live. This information is as necessary for the construction of faith, and learning to live by it, as is any which comes to us out of the Christian tradition.

6. Finally, it is not enough that the five conditions are fulfilled unless they are juxtaposed, put in touch with one another, and there is *conversation* between them. There must be persistent engagement and critical interaction, listening and speaking, putting questions and seeking answers.

I said I would not seek to justify these conditions. It is important to note however that three of them (3, 4 and 5) introduce ways of criticizing as well as building on the kind of confessions of faith mentioned under 2. This is of course essential. The faiths we confess and construct are inevitably limited and relative as we have already said; but more than that, they are also to greater and lesser degrees both false and perverse. False in the sense that we believe or have been taught to believe what isn't true about ourselves or those with whom we live — we have false consciousness. Perverse in that knowingly or unknowingly we believe what benefits us and harms others or harms us all. What people believe is often wrong, misguided, myopic, ideologically self-interested and dangerous. It is not enough to confess it, it must also be constantly criticized. It must come to terms with Jesus Christ, with the contrasting faiths of the great universal church, and with reality as it is and not as we would like or imagine it to be. To accept that we must all have our own faith is not to accept that everyone's faith, or indeed anyone's faith, is true enough and acceptable just as it is. Faith is only constructed by confession and criticism.

The more difficult question concerns the criteria for choosing between one faith and another within the critical conversation. Here I want to make two remarks. First, the most important safeguard against constructing and articulating and learning to live by faiths that are unacceptably limited, parochial, false and perverse is the critical conversation itself. Similarly, the most important safeguard against illegitimate interpretations of the Bible is to put my interpretation alongside that of others. Where people are exposed to different interpretations from their own and to different faiths from their own, questions are raised and alternatives are confronted and there is a good possibility that they will wake up and become aware of how one faith or interpretation can contradict, correct and complement another. But, second, it seems to me a denial of the whole spirit of this enterprise we have called "theology by the people" that criteria for choosing between one faith and another should be imposed on people, any more than a faith or theology should be imposed. If the faith is to be their own, the criteria, beyond those we have mentioned such as Jesus the evangel, must be their own as well. They must decide what their fundamental and over-riding commitments are going to be.

Institutions (including places of work)

I find it important and clarifying to keep in mind these six conditions of theological work when we turn to consider the theme of the consequences of "theology by the people" for institutions and programmes of ministerial formation. Four such institutions are very real in my own theological working life. They are: (a) the local church or congregation; (b) the ordained ministry; (c) programmes of ministerial training and theological education; (d) university faculties of theology; and it had better be made clear that I speak of them as a Baptist living in England, teaching in an English ecumenical federation of colleges and courses, and in an English secular university. My institutions will not be quite the same as yours!

I am going to say very little about the first of these four institutions, the local congregation. We had better remind ourselves, however, that the logical consequence of all our talk about "theology by the people" is to reverse the old batting order. The general assumption has been that the main theological task has been done in the university faculty of theology. That is theology's "place of work". Now we are saying the proper place of theological work is the local church or congregation. It is not done for people and handed down by professionals. It is done by the people, who may of course include professionals, as they gather in community. That means that these communities must fulfill the six conditions we have set out. Some of the basic Christian communities, of which many speak but which few of us have met or belonged to, might fulfill these conditions, but I have to admit that many of the local congregations I have met (and which to Protestant Free Church women and men look remarkably like basic Christian communities at first sight!) do not. They are often pietistic rather than committed to practice; they are, in their activism, surprisingly uninterested in the business of believing; they pay little attention to the Jesus of the Gospels despite their claim to be evangelical; they are parochial rather than catholic; and they persistently turn from worldly realities rather than confront them. I believe there is a mammoth task to be done in converting these communities or, if you like, restoring to them the marks of the church.

Workmates

This need to convert many local congregations into places where the theological tasks of constructing and articulating a faith to live by and learning to live by the faith we have constructed and articulated might be done, raises my next question in an acute form. If people are to do their own theology what help should they be given? The question brings me to one of the oldest and most persistent of Christian institutions, namely the ordained ministry; and here, in a sense, this reflection of mine becomes a case study since one of my major preoccupations in life is helping people to prepare for ordination, and I have not a little interest in discovering whether I have any legitimate reason for continuing to do so. My fear that I may not has one obvious cause in a consultation such as this, since the ordained ministry has all too often been the arch-enemy of theology by the people, seeing itself and being seen by the people as knowing what the faith is, and having the right to tell people what their faith should be and how they should live by it. Is there any hope of the enemy of theology by the people becoming its friend, of ordained ministers becoming the genuine workmates of those who must in the end do the theological tasks for themselves?

I had better make clear what I am about to discuss and what I am not. I am not talking about ministry in general or in any way raising the issue as to whether or not the ministry of the church belongs to all its members. I assume that we all assume that it does. I am not going to discuss the role of so-called professional theologians but that of the ordained minister. I am not going to discuss all the possible roles an ordained minister might be called upon to play, such as leader, enabler, priest, president, pastor; or the ways in which such roles might be justified. I am only going to discuss the contribution the ordained minister might make to the theological tasks of the congregation. Once again I shall not take time justifying my conclusions, only describing them. If I did justify them I should quickly betray my Protestant background where ministers have often been pastoral theologians and teachers, of which I am not altogether ashamed.

Let me repeat that two of the conditions for doing theological work are to pay attention to Jesus, and to all those faiths that have been constructed and articulated and lived by out of loyalty to Jesus. Perhaps I can now refer to all this by the shorthand term: the "common wealth of Christianity". If the theological task is a "do-it-yourself" job, it is not a "do-it-by-yourself" job. If it is local it must never be parochial. What we believe and decide to do must be exposed to what others believe and decide to do. Real heresy is not getting it wrong but getting it wrong in isolation. The task must be done in critical conversation with the common wealth of the church. Could the ordained minister genuinely serve the congregation, or be a workmate in the theological task, by making that common wealth available to the people as best she or he can? If so, that suggests that the ordained minister should know the extent of that wealth or at the very least where it is to be found: in the Bible certainly, but also in the long story of the church with its manifold witnesses to Jesus and its endless confessions of faiths finding expression in liturgies and devotions, books and words and pictures and music, creeds and doctrines, moral codes and stories of faithful obedience. It is this larger and in many ways disturbing set of varied possibilities, and not least the disturbing range of contemporary possibilities, that the ordained minister makes available to the people.

I hope we need not get stuck with the question "why should such a servant of the church be ordained?" though I think there are good reasons why such a servant should be very carefully appointed and authorized as one who is properly equipped to represent the universal and ecumenical life of God's people to the local congregation. If we decide against ordained ministers, something very much like them will always take their place; but the real point of the discussion is whether something very much like these servants with this task does have a proper place.

They are, it should be underlined, separate, identifiable persons, who are looked to as having a special competence and knowledge (and in that sense as being professional) which others do not have. There is a way of talking about "theology by the people" which often implies that all the people should be fit for the theological tasks in much the same way. I am deliberately insisting, because I at least need it clarified, that that is unrealistic, unnecessary and undesirable. Other people will be looked to for competence at other points when it comes to theological work and should not be expected to acquire for themselves the competence which the minister is expected to bring. Such competence may paralyze the laity who have more important things to do.

We must be quite clear however what the competence of this ordained ministry is and what it is not. This workmate brings to the theological task some of the essential tools and building materials for the work. Theological work cannot be done unless the people are exposed to the witnesses to Jesus and the church's many confessions of faith. But having equipped the people to this extent, having opened them up to all the possibilities of faith, the minister is no better placed than any other person in the community to decide what should be made of them when this particular community constructs and articulates its faith and learns to live by it. Indeed there may be others who have the gifts of judgment and discernment in greater measure than the minister; but whatever might turn out to be the case, it is essential to draw the distinction between the minister's competence to put the people in touch with the common wealth of Christianity and the fact that he or she has no right whatsoever to tell the people what in the light of it, and in the light of much else besides, the faith by which they live should be.

I said that I was only going to discuss one ministerial role, but it may be worth adding that the strict limits I have imposed suggest that we should question whether ministers should be leaders of congregations as they have so often been. If equipping people for theological work is different from deciding what the outcome should be, maybe the role of the pastoral theologian is different from that of the leader.

One other footnote: our six conditions for theological work remind us that this ordained minister is not of course the only person needed to equip the people for their theological tasks.

Training for ordained ministry

Bearing in mind that we are not discussing all the roles ministers might play but only their contribution to the theological tasks of the people, it is fairly easy for me to go on to suggest what their training in this respect should be like. I do not intend to spell out a full curriculum, only to register the three main ingredients.

First, ordained ministers need a thorough introduction to the common wealth of Christianity, or as we usually refer to it, the Christian tradition. They need to know of the many testimonies to Jesus and the many forms that faith has taken and now takes, and they need to know why they take the shapes they do, influenced by cultures, historical events and interests. This rather obvious and basic task of learning about the tradition raises many difficult questions about how you do it and about how you select the material, since selection there must be whilst selectivity must be avoided. And even at this early stage we see why such learning must be done in as ecumenical a setting as possible since it is a contradiction in terms for one, biased, narrow, relative Christian tradition to teach itself the wealth of Christianity.

Second, ordained ministers do not only need to know about the tradition, they need to learn how to draw on it as one of the essential resources for the theological tasks of constructing and articulating and learning to live by a faith. Practical theological method is as important as the content of the tradition, but in my experience it is often neglected or relegated to second place. To put it crudely ordinands are given a lot of information but rarely shown what to do with it and how to put it to work. Learning to use the resources cannot of course be left as a rather cold, detached discipline but must come to life in relation to the minister's own attempts to construct and articulate his or her own faith, and learn to live by it.

Third, ordained ministers must be trained to be the workmates of the people, learning how to share with them their knowledge of the rich and varied Christian tradition and helping them to draw on it and make use of it to do their own work. It seems to me that the additional understandings and skills which will be needed here belong to the field of adult education, a discipline which does not feature anything like as prominently as it should in programmes of ministerial training.

Once again, however, the business of actually exposing people to the Christian tradition with its enriching and disturbing possibilities of faith, and of helping them to make use of it, cannot be learned at a distance but only on the job, in company with the people ministers are meant to serve, discovering with them and learning from them how to be of most use. As a result, ministers cannot be properly trained in isolation from the places where theological work is actually done not only by themselves but by the people of God. That is one of the reasons why, in our own training programmes, we have shifted the base of training away from the college or seminary to the local community and the local congregation. Our students for the most part live and work with local communities. They visit the seminary for 36 hours a week. They go to ground for the rest of their time. Once again I have to record that we run into serious difficulties because so often in those congregations the proper working conditions do not exist for getting on with the theological task, and it drives us in some instances to find a base for training outside rather than inside the congregations, where such conditions can become easier to find and people are more committed to practice and open to the realities of the world.

I have spoken about the role of the ordained ministry in relation to the theological tasks of the church, and in very broad outline the content and place of the training needed to prepare them for it. There are of course further hesitations to record. I mention only two. One is very practical. It needs no pointing out that the wealth of Christian tradition (wealth we share and have in common, not a common faith) is virtually limitless. How does an ordained minister even begin to carry such enormous wealth about? In the Bible mainly? In adequate liturgy? In the personal formation of the minister, as well as in information consciously known and shared? If we agree that exposure to this wealth is essential for the theological work of the people, we need to give more thought to how ministers can in practice carry it to them.

The other hesitation is even more serious. This ordained minister is potentially a very powerful figure. We have noted some significant checks on that power. For example other contributions are equally important if theological work has to be done. The minister's voice is by no means the only voice in the conversation suggested by the six marks of the church we have listed. The Bible also is there and open and can be read by many. And it is not for the minister to say what the people's faith should be. Nevertheless the minister has considerable power to decide what to tell the people and what not to tell them, to act as a filter rather than as a funnel when putting them in touch with the wealth of Christianity. And when it comes to drawing on that wealth and using it to construct and live by a faith, the minister is well placed to say how the game should be played and what are legitimate moves, and what are not.

The ministers can even make the game so complicated and esoteric that few others will be able to play it and none as well as they. So the wolf turns up yet again dressed in another set of sheep's clothing and this time does theology for the people by restricting their options and manipulating their decisions. Ministry needs an enormous measure of self-awareness and we need to take seriously the question of proper checks on its considerable power.

Programmes of theological education and university faculties of theology

In focusing attention on ordained ministry and preparation for it I have said little about programmes of theological education, and I only wish to make two remarks about them since so much material is available. One is that I should want to test the adequacy of all patterns of theological education by asking how far they meet the six conditions I have set out for doing theological work. Needless to say extension programmes are not exempt from criticism on this score. The second is that it seems to me that the whole logic of our discussion about theology by the people is to recognize that the main and most important place where theological education takes place is in the local Christian community, without denying that it can for limited purposes take place elsewhere. Tackling the work of constructing and articulating a faith to live by, and learning to live by the faith we have constructed and articulated, *is* in the end the only satisfactory form that theological education can take.

Finally I have said nothing at all about the university faculties of theology, the place where the real theological work has for so long been thought to be done and the really professional theologians might be expected to dwell. All I wish to do now is record my own experience of my own university faculty as a partner in the theological enterprise which for me reaches its proper fulfilment in the theological work of the people of God. I appreciate, not uncritically I hope, three aspects of that partnership. First, the university constantly reminds me of the need for a certain intellectual rigour which we must try to exercise when we do theology with the people just as much as it is exercised in academic institutions. Second, the university may pursue certain enquiries for its own sake or for nobody's sake and certainly not always for the sake of the people, but from which I nevertheless benefit and on which I am to some extent parasitic, as it investigates the texts and uncovers the content and nature of the Christian tradition and common wealth in a way for which I have neither the equipment nor the time but the results of which I am anxious to use. Third, the university may not always be as responsive to the church as one would like, dutifully setting about those tasks which the church judges to be most helpful at this particular point in its pilgrimage; but I am disposed to think that at times it fulfills its responsibility by being somewhat irresponsible and producing material which is not what the church could have judged to be most relevant, so jolting its perspectives from an independent point of view. The university faculty can too easily be removed from the committed practice and obedience of God's people to be the place where their theological work is done, but it remains for me a companion, as ambiguous as all the rest of us, that I would not wish to be without.

So this paper is an invitation to discuss *first* the adequacy of the six conditions I have outlined for doing theological work, for congregational life and for patterns of theological education; *second*, what help people need to do their theological work; and *third* who, including ministers or pastors, might be expected to help, what roles they should play and what training they require.

XIII

An Open Letter to Colleagues
in Theological Education

Gathered by the Programme on Theological Education of the World Council of Churches from different regions, cultures, and traditions, we are people concerned with theological education. Committed to engage and prepare the church for hearing and responding to God's call in our times, we have grappled with the theme "Theology by the People". We want to share with you our first learnings and invite your contributions as we continue to seek God's leading for our ministries.

We have seen more sharply in recent years that God's good news is being proclaimed among the poor and by the poor — women and men and children and youth who are marginalized, oppressed, exploited, and dehumanized in many ways — as a message of liberation, justice, and fullness of life. This is good news for all people, for our humanity is fulfilled by seeking fulfilment for all God's people. This focus on the poor has cultural, economic, political, social, and spiritual dimensions, for it is a vision of the abundant life which God in Christ intends for us all. It opens to us an understanding of the evils of our times and provides access to the spiritual power that can transform lives, renew the life of the church, and form new social institutions. It offers hope for those who work for justice and peace in the midst of secularism and militarism under the shadow of nuclear holocaust.

Because our world is so filled with oppression, alienation, and impoverishment, we believe that all people, especially the oppressed-poor, are called by God's Spirit to articulate their own theology as they discover that the God of the Bible is on their side and as we all resist the principalities and overcome the forces of death. Theology is the task of the people who become critically conscious in communities of faith and action. We have seen dynamic and diverse expressions of people's theology among base communities in Latin America and Europe, movements of women and minorities in North America and Australia-New Zealand, vital Christian communities in Africa, groups struggling for their rights and dignity in Asia and the Pacific, sisters and brothers with disabilities, and others who weep and celebrate through ancient and modern liturgies. We believe that they will increasingly enrich and inspire the world Christian community, the wider family of faiths, and the whole human community which yearns for fulfilment.

As we consider our task as theological educators, we are humbled before God and before God's people. We now see more clearly that we must learn to listen to the stories of suffering people as they tell of their hope and work for justice in the midst of oppression. We need to learn their language, interpret their experiences and stories for ourselves and others in the light of the gospel, and make available to them the experience of the universal church, the wisdom of the Christian tradition, and appropriate critical tools.

We need to learn to read the Bible not only with the tools of scholarship but also through the eyes of the poor and the marginalized, in order to understand God's message and make our response as disciples of Jesus Christ. We need to be changed in accordance with this understanding.

We feel the need to shape our institutions and programmes of theological education in ways that will enable all who participate to become companions of the poor in their struggles and also enable our churches and societies to hear and respond to their cry.

We know that there will always be many different ways to undertake theological education, and we rejoice that many creative efforts have already been made to carry out our mandate closer to local congregations and communities. But we sense that God's compassion for the poor is a newly urgent priority for theological education. We suggest that this will require new relationships between theological studies and social realities, church traditions and people's movements, spiritual discipline and cultural roots, learning and suffering, pastors and congregations within the body of Christ, which was broken that all might have life.

We invite you to share your experiences and reflections as we seek together to reshape our vision for theological education. We send you our greetings and wish for you God's blessings as brothers and sisters in Christ.

Appendix I

Coming under the Discipline of the Word: Three Experiences

1. The *Community of Cassano*, Naples, went through various phases of Bible reading which are instructive for the development of the grassroots relationship to the Bible.

First phase: There was individual reading of the Bible, and the community served as an instrument to share each one's personal reflections. The approach was fundamentalist. Everything was based on personal intuitions and individual inspiration. Encounter with the Bible represented a period of prayer and meditation aimed at improving personal relationships, and the life of each individual. The gain had been the break in the chains of institutional church mediation (often manipulation) and the acquiring of some personal capacity for analysis and interpretation. This process, however, tended to mean looking for messages in the Bible which were pleasing to the person or the community. Behind the approach lay an unspoken conviction that the Bible was the perfect book, written once for all, and as such required no historical-scientific instruments in order to be understood.

There was also an attempt to develop a traditional but participative eucharistic celebration: but none of the priests were prepared to work on such a basis. The type of action the group engaged in was that which showed solidarity, covering juvenile detenion homes, aid to laid-off workers, investigation of bad housing.

Second phase: The community then began to use, as instruments, books which were rigorously critical about the biblical material. It came to the point where "the experts" (now books) were considered to provide the final word — even with regard to fundamental questions underlying everything else. "We are not conscious of it — but we had still been delegating the interpretative dimension of the Bible to others," they confessed.

At this stage, the community was searching for an alternative way of celebrating the eucharist, and questioning all welfare forms of charity. The community's socio-political engagement was aimed essentially at protesting against a church which was an instrument of power.

Third phase: The community came to recognize that the Bible was written in a specific historical situation, by people of a given historical period, which had a particular culture and goals. It was necessary to make the Bible live in the present human situation. The community made the following affirmation: "None of us intends to delegate to others, to external authorities, the task of interpreting the biblical message for our lives. We and we alone can and must discover the sense that the scriptures hold for our personal growth and our daily praxis. Refusal to delegate the interpretation of the relationship of the word of God to today's history is the fundamental underlying element of our reappropriation of the scriptures."

In order that the word of God might be reappropriated by the poor, the community found it necessary to live the condition of the poor — not by identifying with them but participating concretely in their liberation struggles. They believed that this perspective was necessary if the message was to be lived in a non-alienating way.

At present, their concerns are centred on the proclamation of the word of God. They have rejected the idea of transmitting to others a personal interpretation of the word of God; and, even more firmly, proselytism. They see the natural locus for proclamation as the multiplicity of possibilities for encounter-dialogue-confrontation available in daily life.

2. The *Christian Grassroots Community of Oregina* (Genoa) has listed certain discoveries regarding community Bible reading. This represents *encounter-dialogue* over problems and truths previously tackled either by individuals or their families.

— *The discovery* of group work and reflection as instruments for the collective growth of conscience.
— *The acquisition* of strength and courage in place of the traditional mediaeval fears which hierarchical authoritarianism has inculcated in each individual.
— *The discovery* of critical reasoning as a value, condition and instrument for moving towards freedom.
— *Fresh awareness* that the Bible (and the same is true for our conscience and our words) is the object of a manipulation which the hierarchical power has exercised through history, utilizing repressive

organizations, laws and institutions; and that there will be no completeness for the human person until these anti-human institutions have been uprooted or substituted.

— A *flowing together* of the biblical text and world reality.

The method of Bible study at present is to use small groups — which draw together, in writing, the reflections of the members. Where themes intersect and show a convergence of thinking, they are rediscussed and periodically studied in depth. This method does not prevent the adoption of thought-patterns which are *not* derived from people's creative reflection, but from the dominant ideology.

It is recognized that the use of the Bible itself, in the past, has been aimed at effecting a kind of slavery. Signs of restoration of justice must accompany the reading of the message. The Oregina group was composed of a few hundred families and two ex-Franciscan priests, and its outreach was national.

3. The *Group of San Voghera* (Pavia) is a community of about 50 persons, mostly between 17 and 28 years of age, formed around the local parish priest.

The group started by following the normal Sunday readings; but became aware that this produced a static, vague message.

Next, two people and the priest were asked to look into the historical situation of the first Corinthian Christians. But the community became aware that it was still delegating to others what should be a common responsibility. It also lacked study materials.

A group of the community was then mandated to undertake a work of exegesis and presentation. But few were able to incarnate the word of God in daily experience. Some advance was made when the community divided itself into four groups to follow up a fundamental theme concerning the experience of the prophet Jeremiah. The community attempted to make a map of the social conflicts at that period of history. At the same time they developed a dialogue-homily at the heart of the mass. Present problems of society, public sector housing, feminism, etc., were brought into sharp relationship with the text of Jeremiah. People had not prepared themselves adequately to do a serious job on this; they found themselves called to an active role after centuries of passivity.

In July 1979, the community was deprived of the use of the parish meeting hall, and was forbidden to speak at the mass. Disorientation inevitably followed. However, Sunday readings were resumed: and conviction regarding the usefulness of digging into the social-economic-political insights in the Bible resurfaced. They began to read Girardet and the Belo[1] and did continuous Bible reading from their perspective. However there were still risks.

1. A commentary might be accepted as more than it was — simply one attempt to understand scripture; it might be treated as the equivalent of scripture itself.

2. People could passively take what they read — without fighting it out with the text and without incarnating into daily life what came from confrontation with the word of God.

3. The community could accept the use of a language which was incomprehensible to the majority of the people. (Only such terms should be employed as are understood and used by all the community.)

4. There was the constant temptation to delegate to others responsibility for digging into the biblical message.

Note: "Materialistic" exegesis of the Bible is one in which study includes the social relationships created by the then existing economy, and its influence on the political and especially the cultural and ideological frameworks of thought and practices of that period. An attempt is then made to pinpoint the forms of conflict existing between the various strata of society; and finally to evaluate the way in which the word of God was directed towards the oppressed, the poor and the imprisoned.

IAN FRASER

---

[1] Expositors of a materialist reading of the Bible.

Appendix II
Select Bibliography

African theology

Appiah-Kubi, K. and Torres, S., eds, *African Theology en Route*, New York, Maryknoll, 1972.

Dickson, K.A., *Theology in Africa*, New York, Orbis, 1984.

Idown, E. Bolagi, *Towards an Indigenous Church*, London, OUP, 1985.

Ilogu, E., *Christianity and Igbo Culture*, London, E.J. Brill, 1974.

Kato, B.H., *Theological Pitfalls in Africa*, Kisumu, Evangel Publishing, 1975.

Mbiti, J.S., *New Testament Eschatology in an African Background*, London, OUP, 1972.

Mulago, V., *Un visage africain du christianisme*, Paris, Présence africaine, 1965.

Pobee, J.S., *Toward an African Theology*, Nashville, Abingdon, 1979.

Sawyer, H., *Creative Evangelism*, London, Lutterworth, 1968.

Asian theology

Abayasekera, J. and Niles, P., eds, *For the Dawning of the News*, Singapore, CTC-CCA, 1981.

Boyd, Robin, *Kristadvaita: Theology for India*, Madras, Christian Literature Society, 1977.

Bulletin of the Commission on Theological Concerns, Christian Conference of Asia: CCTC Volume No. 2 1984, Volume No. 3 1984.

Carr, Dhyanchand, *Gospel through Dissent*, Madurai, T.T. Seminary, 1985.

CCTC, ed., *Minjung Theology*, Singapore, CCA/Maryknoll, Orbis, 1983.

England, John, ed., *Living Theologies in Asia*, London, SCM, 1981.

Fabella, Virginia, ed., *Asia's Struggle for Full Humanity*, Maryknoll, Orbis, 1980.

Ileto, R.C., *Pasyon and Revolution*, Manila, 1970.

Kim Chi Ha, *The Gold Crowned Jesus and Other Writings*, Maryknoll, Orbis, 1978.

Kim Jong Bock, ed., *Asia Forum on Justice and Development*, Singapore, CCA/CCPD, 1984.

Koyama, Kosuke, *Water Buffalo Theology*, Singapore, SPCK, 1970.

Niles, Preman and Thomas, T.K., eds, *Varieties of Witness*, Singapore, CCA, 1980.
Song, C.S., *The Third Eye Theology*, Maryknoll, Orbis, 1979.
Song, C.S., *The Compassionate God*, Maryknoll, Orbis, 1979.
Theologie des gottes Volkes in Sud Korea, Neuekirchenes, 1984.

Black theology
Becken, H.J., ed., *Relevant Theology for Africa*, Durban, Lutheran Publishing House, 1973.
Boesak, Allan, *Farewell to Innocence: a Socio-Ethical Study on Black Theology and Power*, Maryknoll, Orbis, 1977.
Cone, James H., *Black Theology and Black Power*, New York, Seabury, 1969.
Cone, James H., *A Black Theology of Liberation*, Philadelphia, Lippincott, 1970.
Cone, James H., *Gospel of the Oppressed*, New York, Seabury, 1975.
Moore, Basil, ed., *The Challenge of Black Theology in South Africa*, Atlanta, John Knox, 1974.
Moore, Basil, ed., *Black Theology: the South African Voice*, London, Hurst & Co., 1973.
Torres, S. and Fabella, Virginia, eds, *The Emergent Gospel: Theology from the Underside of History*, Maryknoll, Orbis, 1978.

Latin American theology
Boff, Leonardo, *Jesu Cristo Libertador*, translated into English as *Jesus Christ Liberator: a Critical Christology for Our Times*, Maryknoll, Orbis, 1978.
Boff, Leonardo, *Eclesiognese*, Petropolis, Vezes, 1978 (English translation: *Eclesiogenesis*).
Boff, L. and Elizondo, Virgil, eds, *The People of God and the Poor*, Edinburgh, Clark, 1984.
Cardenal, Ernesto, *The Gospel in Solantiname*, Maryknoll, Orbis, 1976.
Castillo, Fernando, *Theologie aus der Praxis der Volkes: Neuere Studien zum Lateinamerikanischen Christentum und zur Theology der Befreiung*, Munich, Kaiser, 1978.
Cussianovich, Alejandro, *Religious Life and the Poor: Liberation Theology Perspectives*, Maryknoll, Orbis, 1979 (translated from *Desde los Pobres de la Tierra*).
Gutiérrez, Gustavo, *A Theology of Liberation: History, Politics and Salvation*, New York, Orbis, 1973 (translated from *Teología de la Liberación*).
Gutiérrez, Gustavo, *La Fuerza Histórica de los Pobres*, Lima, CEP, 1979 (English translation: *The Historical Power of the Poor*).
Reiser, Antonio, ed., *Basisgemeinden und Befreiung*, Wuppertal, Jugenddienst Verlag, 1981.
Richard, Pablo, *La Iglesia de los Pobres en America Central*, San José, DEI, 1982.

Santa Ana, Julio de, *Good News to the Poor: the Challenge of the Poor in the History of the Church*, Maryknoll, Orbis, 1979.

Sedoc, eds, *Una Iglesia que Nace del Pueblo*, Salamanca, Sigueme, 1979.

Segundo, Juan Luis, *Liberation of Theology*, Maryknoll, Orbis, 1976 (translated from *Liberación de la Teología*).

Sobrino, Jon, *Resurrección de la Verdadera Iglesia*, Espana, Sal Terra, 1981 (English translation: *The True Church and the Poor*).

Torres, Sergio and Fabella, Virginia, eds, *The Challenge of the Basic Christian Communities*, Maryknoll, Orbis, 1974.

Appendix III
Participants

Prof. Jean-Pierre Bastian
San Jeronimo 111
Mexico, D.F. 0100
Mexico

Rev. Agustin Batlle
P.O. Box 21570
Nairobi
Kenya

Ms Nansie Blackie
St Colm's College
23 Inverleith Terrace
Edinburgh, EH3 5NX
United Kingdom

Prof. Dr Peter C. Bloth
Troppauer Strasse 6A
1000 Berlin 45
German Democratic Republic

Prof. François Bovon
chemin de la Paix
1261 Genolier
Switzerland

Bunug
c/o Don Carrington
P.O. Box 40371
Casuarian 5792
Australia

Lic. E. Jorge Bravo Caballero
Paseo Colón 209
Lima 1
Peru

Rev. Raul Pedro Cardoso
c/o Camacua 282
1406 Buenos Aires
Argentina

Rev. Don Carrington
P.O. Box 40371
Casuarina 5792
Australia

Mr Raul Vidales Delgado
Pacifico 517
C201 Coyoacan
Mexico

Dr Enrique Dussel
Celayan 21-402
06100 Mexico D.F.
Mexico

Ms Agneta Enermalm-Ogawa
Stormgatan 1
75431 Uppsala
Sweden

Rev. Wilfredo Estrado Adorno
Colegio Bíblico Pentecostal de Puerto Rico
Box 8, Saint Just
Puerto Rico 00750
USA

Rev. Dr Ian M. Fraser
Ferndale
Gargunnock FK8 3BW
Scotland
United Kingdom

Rev. Dr John Robert Gaden
Trinity College
Parkville, Vic. 3052
Australia

Mrs Ana Langerak de Garcia
CEPAD, Apartado 3091
Managua
Nicaragua 1406

Prof. Dr Adriaan Geense
Ecumenical Institute
Chateau de Bossey
1298 Celigny
Switzerland

Dr Hellmut E. Gnadt
Casilla 13596
Santiago
Chile

Dr Enrique Guang
Apartado 3977
San José
Costa Rica

Dr James W. Gunn
20 John Cava Lane
Peekskill, NY 10566
USA

Mr Andres Miranda Hernandez
Canarias No. 18B
San Simon
Mexico DF 03660
Mexico

Mr Manuel Hernandez Mondaca
Casilla 2341
Correo Concepción
Chile

Prof. Vasil I. Istavridis
Yeni Yuva Sok No. 40/3
Cihangir/Beyoglu
Istanbul
Turkey

Prof. Mikhail Ivanov
Zagorsk, Lavra
USSR

Dr C. Douglas Jay
Emmanuel College
75 Queens Park Crescent
Toronto M5S 1R7
Canada

Dr E.C. John
17 Miller's Road
Bangalore 560 046
India

Rt Rev. William A. Jones
1210 Locust St.
St Louis, MO 63103
USA

Ms Rita Khater
Ron Point Ajaltour
IMM Nabih Khater
Ajaltoun
Lebanon

Rev. Preston Telford Kelsey
Executive Director
Board for Theological Education
815 Second Avenue
New York, NY 10017
USA

Dr F. Ross Kinsler
2608 N. Boulder Road
Altadena, CA 91001
USA

Rev. Joshua N. Kudadjie
Dept. for the Study of Religion
University of Ghana
P.O. Box 66
Legon
Ghana

Dr Peter Kuzmic
B.T.I., Kosirnikova 76
41000 Zagreb
Yugoslavia

Mr Eduardo Lopez
c/o Cree, Casilla 8087
Quito
Ecuador

Rev. Pascual Mamani
Casilla 356
La Paz
Bolivia

Dr Jaci Maraschin
Rua Rego Freitas
530 E-13 Aste
01220 Sao Paulo S.P.
Brazil

Mgr Francesco Marchisano
Sacred Congregation for Catholic
Education, 3 Piazza Pio XII
00193 Rome
Italy

Rev. Odén Marichal Rodriguez
Apartado 149
Matanzas
Cuba

Prof. Alberto Moisés Mendez-Ulloa
San Jeronimo 137
Col San Angel
01000 Mexico D.F.
Mexico

Dr Luis Fidel Mercado
776 Ponce de Leon Avenue
Hato Ray
Puerto Rico 00918
USA

Rev. Sientje Merentek-Abram
P.O. Box 4, Tomohon
Sulut
Indonesia

Ms Isabel Apawo Migochi
Chancellor College
P.O. Box 280
Zomba
Malawi

Prof. José Miguez-Bonino
212 Clifton Road
Atlanta, GA 30307
USA

Rev. Dr Howard M. Mills
United Theological Seminary
of the Twin Cities
3000 Fifth St., N.W.
New Brighton, MN 55112
USA

Fr Peter Miria
Holy Spirit Seminary
P.O. Box 1717
Boroko
Papua New Guinea

Dr Rafel Murillo
La Tolfeca 69
Mexico D.F.
Mexico

Dr Anna Mathilda Nagelschmidt
Avenida Higienopolis 360
Apartado 63
Sao Paulo
Brazil

Rev. Iqbal Nisar
P.O. Box 13
Gujranwala
Pakistan

Dr Levi Oracion
Union Theological Seminary
P.O. Box 841
Manila
Philippines

Rev. Dr A.H. Harry Oussoren
Room 213, 85 St Claire Avenue E.
Toronto, Ontario M4T 1M8
Canada

Mr Salatiel Palomino
Sem. Juan Calvino Cuauhtemoc 117
Carmen Coyoacan
Cp. 004100
Mexico D.F.
Mexico

Dr Nyanza-Nzambi Paluku Rubiga
B.P. 988
Bangui
Central African Republic

Dr Jorge Pixley
Av. San Jéronimo 137
San Angel 01000
Mexico D.F.
Mexico

Ms Maria Teresa Porcile-Santiso
Av. Luis P. Ponce 1563/67
Montevideo
Uruguay

Rev. Horacio Prado
Casilla 3798
Quito
Ecuador

Mr José M. Ramirez
SLB, Apartado 901
San José
Costa Rica

Drs Anneke Ravestein
Ecumenical Institute
Chateau de Bossey
1298 Céligny
Switzerland

Prof. Paulo Ricco
Via Pietro Cossa 42
00193 Rome
Italy

Mr Daniel Rodriguez
San Jeronimo 137
01000 Mexico D.F.
Mexico

Lic. Norberto Saracco
Camacua 282, Asit
1406 Buenos Aires
Argentina

Mr Raul Serradel Romero
Fco Selpaso, yT 248-A-6
V. Carranza
15900 Mexico D.F.
Mexico

Dr Milton Schwantes
Av. Nazaré 993
04263 Sao Paulo S.P.
Brazil

Dr Ingram S. Seah
Taiwan Theological College
20 Lane 2, sec. 2
Yan Teh Highway
Shihlin, Taipei
Taiwan

Rev. Prof. David Kwang-Sun-Suh
126-22 Daeshin-Dong
Suhdaemoon-Ku
Seoul
South Korea

Mrs Elsa Tamez
Apartado 901
1000 San José
Costa Rica

Rev. Dr Michael Hugh Taylor
Northern Baptist College
Brighton Grove
Rusholme
Manchester M14 5JP
United Kingdom

Mrs Tatiana Tchernikova
Ryleev Str. 18/2
Moscow
USSR

Rev. Canon Noel Titus
Codrington College
St John
Barbados
West Indies

Rev. I. Sevati Tuwere
P.O. Box 388
Suva
Fiji

Dr Procoro F. Velasques
P.O. Box 5002
Rudge Ramos
Sâo Bernardo do Campo, S.P.
Brazil

Rev. Dr Mary Kathryn Weir
Vancouver School of Theology
6000 Fona Avenue
Vancouver B.C. V6T 1L4
Canada

Rev. Dietrich Werner
Auf der Höhe 19
D-2903 Bad Zwischenahn
Federal Republic of Germany

Rev. Haydn O. White
Room 1249
475 Riverside Drive
New York, NY 10015
USA

Dr Chook-Lak Yeow
4 Mount Sophia
Singapore 0922

Mr Amzie Yoder
Director, Semilla
Apartado 1779
Guatemala City
Guatemala

Rev. Roger Zavala
Apartado 2555
Managua
Nicaragua

Dr Barbara Brown Zikmund
Pacific School of Religion
1798 Scenic Avenue
Berkeley, CA 94709
USA

Staff
Rev. Dr Samuel Amirtham
Ms Joann Nash Eakin
Ms Rose-Marie Extermann
Prof. John S. Pobee